Embarrassed

*Living with a faith that makes
no sense to my friends*

— GRAHAM TURNER —

Sacristy
Press

Sacristy Press
PO Box 612, Durham, DH1 9HT

www.sacristy.co.uk

First published in 2025 by Sacristy Press, Durham

Sacristy Limited, registered in England & Wales, number 7565667

British Library Cataloguing-in-Publication Data
A catalogue record for the book is available from the British Library

ISBN 978-1-78959-367-9

To my brother Andrew (1951–2019)
who taught me more than I ever realized.

Also by Graham Turner

God's People and the Seduction of Empire (Sacristy Press, 2016)
Alternative Collects (Sacristy Press, 2018)
Seeing Luke Differently (2021)
Seeing John Differently (2022)
Seeing Mark Differently (2023)

*To believe in something
and not to live it is dishonest.*
MAHATMA GANDHI

*Be yourself;
everyone else is already taken.*
OSCAR WILDE

Contents

Acknowledgements

My African friends say it takes a village to raise a child. Well, it takes a lot of people to get a book to publication. Without my "village" of friends this project would never have come to fruition.

I am grateful to David Black who pushed me to write this memoir and has travelled the whole distance through some rough drafts and uncertainties. John Bleazard pointed me in the right direction to discover the importance of story-telling that had somehow passed me by for much of my life, and Ian Dawson (sadly missed) who helped me think clearly about science. Mark Waters linked me with people who could help me as did Michael Connaughton. Thank you for being allies I can trust.

There has also been the wonderful band of draft script readers who have examined my text at its various stages to make comments on its content, structure, spelling and grammar. Judith Whittingham, Rob Crawford, Glenys Chalk, Paul and Lynne Spedding, Nick Easton and Jonathan Stockdale are all part of my village. Thank you for being there for me and giving me crucial and honest feedback.

So many people have enriched my life over the years and been alongside me as I've tried to figure out my direction and purpose. Your stories are interwoven with my story; you may well recognize yourself in parts of this book. (Some names have been changed to protect the privacy of certain individuals.) Thank you for making my life story rich.

Most of all, I am grateful to Rosie, my life partner, friend and companion who has always believed in the importance of telling stories, and that I must tell mine. You have shaped my life, for good, more than any other person. Thank you for believing in me and giving me the space to get this job done.

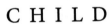

CHILD

1

The secret

My troubles started on the Bible Belt of south Manchester, a string of churches that believed only they, and those like them, were right.

I was born the third child of four. With Mum and Dad, we were a good half-dozen, well-connected and secure.

Faith in our neck of the woods was a mixture of courage and arrogance, wisdom and naivety. This only became a problem just before I entered my teens. Then, I began to harbour a secret that has persisted my whole life—until now.

Over the decades, I've wrestled with this secret, understood it better and eventually learned to befriend it. But now is the time for my "coming out". It has become a matter of integrity. If I don't speak about this, then I won't have been honest with you. If I haven't been honest with you, I won't have been honest with myself.

I've been a vicar in the Church of England for over 35 years, making a living from peddling the "Jesus faith" of the Bible. Yet despite this, I've disliked the label "Christian", a dislike that occasionally bordered on revulsion. Whenever a friend or acquaintance realized I was one, I wanted to run and hide. I was embarrassed. I wanted to be someone else.

This embarrassment blighted me from the age of 11. I battled with it when I repeatedly tried to do what was right, even as a vicar.

What follows is the story of my struggle with the dis-ease that has haunted me from its dark shadows. At times, it felt worse than embarrassment; it felt like shame. It also felt like fear.

You may ask, what is so shameful about being a Christian?

Well, according to many who don't believe, we God-fearers are odd. We're said to believe all sorts of peculiar, dangerous and stupid doctrines. For instance, it is only us churchy types who are going to heaven, while everybody else is off to hell to burn in a well-stoked incinerator.

Many avoid us. Others feel sorry for us. Some think we're simple-minded, moralizing prudes who are more against life than for it. They assume we're opposed to evolution, a good time, sex, doubt, satire and alcohol. They roll their eyes when they hear Christians ask God for a space in a crowded car park. They suspect we are all in favour of asking the Almighty to arrange a hot sunny day for our trip to the seaside while others are desperate for rain.

We're the ones responsible for making people feel guilty when they swear in front of us, so much so they feel obliged to apologize. Many think we all love church buildings, organs and robed choirs. They suspect we adore stained-glass windows and brass rubbing and consider Gothic or Victorian architecture beautiful. Not all of us do.

Our weird church worlds are (or used to be) populated by men in dresses. Some wear funny pointed hats while others covet titles as they compete to see who is more "reverend". We're denounced as stuck in an old, boring and irrelevant world. In this batty, dumb and futile world, we adherents are considered too heavenly-minded to be of any earthly use.

These non-believers pity us. They think we worship a sky-God, a Zeus-like being, who rules over a three-decker universe. They assume we are stuck in a "flat earth" belief system. In this universe, various other dubious gods and angelic beings exist above the clouds to rule and manage the world, as if the whole of reality is a gargantuan war-based video game.

In this supposed "dark and evil" world portrayed by the Christians, humans must learn to avoid these dubious gods to follow the one true God. This true God is better, greater and more potent than the rest of them put together.

It is in this alternative reality that we believers get offended when some comedian takes a pop at our religious beliefs. We leap to God's defence in case he (after all, "He" is a he, isn't he?) is not up to the job.

Well, who wouldn't feel on edge when accused of this load of peculiarity?

Despite all this, I've tried to follow the Middle Eastern Jesus, who, like an old habit, I cannot give up.

This story, of my long-held embarrassment, isn't about the many issues paraded in the press. It isn't about the church's attitude to sexual abuse, the mistreatment of gays, trans people and those of colour. It isn't about our collusion in the slave trade or how we've sided with corrupt power. All these are atrocious. But they've been well catalogued and aired by voices better than mine. Don't get me wrong, reader, these significant issues are much more devastating than my private angst. Still, they don't render my experience invalid. My story adds to the picture of a faith I treasure despite its many warts and serious blemishes.

Carrying this disquiet has made me feel weak and deficient. I've shrunk back from the sticky Christian branding whenever I've ended up chatting with those who don't do church. I'm talking here about sceptics, atheists, agnostics, antagonists, humanists, secularists, pagans, and any with little sympathy for people of faith.

I've now come to the point where I want to be honest about my turmoil and struggle, my heavy backpack of shame. If I can be honest, I believe I will have done something of value.

Suffering and struggle have a strange effect on you. This secret I've harboured for over 50 years has made me fear. It has inhibited me. But at the same time, it has also emboldened me and opened doors that would otherwise have remained closed.

My good friend David Black started me out on this writing venture. I told him about my chronic angst. I told him I felt unable to explain my predicament to my non-faith friends. He got straight to the point. "You need to tell it as a story. I'd like to hear your story. I'd like to hear how you arrived at where you are today; it interests me." But alas, I'm no storyteller, I pleaded. I'm an explainer. My engineering training taught me to analyse and interpret.

Later, when talking to R at home, I relayed my defensive conversation with David. She was clear. "I agree with him; he's right. You need to share your story; I like stories, not explanations." (It's true. She often looks blank when I attempt to explain an idea or concept I've come up with.) She added, "Lots of people like to hear a story."

So, the die was cast. My fate was sealed. They told me what I must do; I had to write. I had to find out how to do what I'd convinced myself I couldn't do.

Late in the day, I have realized life is all about stories. We learn by hearing them and sharing them. It's a human thing. We don't understand so well through ideas and concepts, despite what I'd thought all my life. It took a nudge from David to make me figure this out. Now I understand. We communicate what is essential through chatter, gossip and laughter-making.

As a flute player, I ride out of town each week with a car full of other musicians for our band's rehearsal. We talk and laugh for half an hour as we travel. It's all stories, of course.

A new church member once told me, "No one belongs until their story has been heard." They understood this because they were new. Well, I want to tell you mine; then maybe I'll belong more deeply to you and you to me.

This book, though, doesn't tell you everything about me. It is a vein running through my life. It is a vein that has hampered me and held me back. But it is also the fault line that has sent me digging to see if anything richer lies hidden. This book is about living with a tension. I've wanted to be a follower of a first-century Palestinian maverick, yet I've also found many things about Christianity embarrassing, awkward and exasperating.

My sometimes-arbitrary route through life has, at times, made me sad and left me feeling alone. But hey, don't cry for me. Don't pity me or seek to come over and smother me with your nicefulness. No. Without this disruption, I'd never have learned what I now know. Without this, my life wouldn't be as meaningful as it is today. Without this, I would've become the worst sort of priggish religious type. I would've gloated about being on the superior side of a falsely divided reality. Don't cry for me; I wouldn't have it any other way. My journey has been a gift.

While I've felt unique in my awkwardness, I'm not special. Many have had a similar experience. Their names could have been on the front of this book. I've found life-long friends in such people. They are the unshockable types who look at me sideways when I mouth off about another of my pet grumbles. But I know they love me. They provoke me to go away and come back with a more coherent and wise perspective. These are the people who carry a similar dis-ease. They've encouraged me to keep exploring for something else. They, too, want a faith that doesn't turn our non-church friends against us without good reason.

Many have travelled with this mixture of joy and discomfort, an emulsion of being that never seems to rest comfortably with itself. I'm not special, at least in this. They, like me, appreciate and enjoy so much that is *not* church or religion.

I have to recount what follows, even if it is just for a few to hear. It is for those who see me from the outside and know little of where I get my energy.

I must tell this for those who are a part of me, without whom my existence would fall like a pack of cards. Without them, I wouldn't be very much *me*.

But I've also written this for a special group of you, those whom I regard as my non-religious friends, acquaintances, colleagues and contacts. It is for those who've looked at me quizzically as if to say, "You seem like an okay sort of guy, how come you believe all this crazy Christian nonsense?"

As I grew up, I was led to believe my faults, failures and weaknesses would lead me into the cul-de-sacs of life. But I found this isn't true. I needed these many wrong turnings; they were necessary diversions. They made me sit up and pay attention as I sped my way along. Without these disruptions, I'd never have found my path to what I now believe is a better place.

If what follows enlightens you even in some small way, it will have been worth the effort. If it enhances our friendship and contributes to our mutual understanding, then so much the better.

It all started on the south Manchester Bible Belt a little before I entered my teens. This was when I began to harbour my secret. But let me tell you first where I emerged from.

2

Surveillance God

From as far back as I can remember, God was always knocking around our place—at least, that's who they said it was. He lurked in doorways, listening to what was being said, watching all that happened. It could all be a bit spooky.

Looking back, it wasn't hard to regard our small world as somewhat sinister. It felt as if God operated as a secret policeman—KGB/FSB style—but in a more kindly manner.

Propaganda hung on our walls, reinforcing the accepted Christian message. Placed just inside our front room was a velvet-covered board. Embossed on it in gold letters was a message for family and visitors to take note of:

CHRIST IS THE HEAD
of this house
THE UNSEEN GUEST
at every meal
THE SILENT LISTENER
to every conversation

When I was young, this wasn't a problem as I couldn't read. But over time, the words (especially those in capitals) started to mess with my head. I began to attach meanings and feelings to them, meanings and feelings which weren't always welcome. I sat many an hour on the sofa with those words bearing down on me. They made me curious; they also made me fearful. They made me question. Why did this Christ not talk? Where did he sit at mealtimes? Our table was always quite full, with the six of us crammed around it, often with an extra guest or two. Taking things at face value is the gift of a child.

The mystery was even greater in the back room. On the wall opposite the fireplace was a wooden plaque, a gift from a missionary returning from the "mission field". Its stark black gloss lettering on a slab of mahogany read:

> Before you call
> I will answer
> *Isaiah 65:24*

This was more than confusing. Where does one start when the end appears before the beginning? How would the person speaking (presumably THE SILENT LISTENER of the front room) guess what I wanted until I'd mentioned it? Staring at this as a child seemed to lock my brain into a merry-go-round I couldn't escape. It didn't make sense. It couldn't make sense.

Being looked upon by God was a strong theme in the Christianity my family swam in. But, if it was okay for Mum and Dad, then I assumed it would be okay for me.

Mum and Dad were my place of safety in the middle of our God-inhabited house. They were trying to do what was right in a world dominated by Cold War news, news which informed us we were in danger of collapsing into a nuclear soup.

Each Sunday, following the morning service, we'd usually tuck into a roast lamb dinner. (The cut of meat we enjoyed was always an indicator of the family's finances that week: leg if all was well, shoulder if the budget was a bit on the tight side.) Then, we children were packed off to Sunday School while Mum and Dad had a child-free hour asleep in the front room.

Being observed was also a dominant message when we gathered in the church halls on those afternoons. The teaching burrowed its way into my head as I developed from the chrysalis of my infancy. As fear dug its way into my consciousness, so did its close cousin, guilt. Week by week, along with another hundred or so pliable minds, I sang jaunty songs that reinforced the party line.

O be careful little hands what you do.
O be careful little hands what you do.
There's a Father up above
who is looking down in love.
O be careful little hands what you do.[1]

We sang this full of belief and enthusiasm. Each verse rolled on from the other to ensure that no arena of human activity was missed. We had to be careful what our little eyes saw, what our little ears heard, where our little feet walked, what our little hands touched and what our little tongues said. As little people living in sight of our surveillance God, we had to be careful to be careful.

I had no idea the impact such a repetitive message was having on my delicate conscience as I evolved from the wonderful state of not-knowing into what I would become.

Being looked at all the time can't be good for anyone. We all need a bit of privacy to try out things we're not sure are okay. Stepping over prescribed boundaries is necessary for a maturing sense of self, isn't it? I needed to discover what it might feel like to transgress at times. Now, some things were best not tried (like murder or laughing at Grandpa when he farted). But I wouldn't know what other things felt like unless I had a go (like eating sugar for breakfast or rummaging through my parents' private things in their bedside cabinet). At times, telling the difference between right and wrong was straightforward. Then, at other times, it was hard to figure out.

As I started to break free of my chrysalis (to become more moth than butterfly), I didn't doubt there was a God, just as I didn't doubt the baker's shop called Mathers sold the sweet bread, Sally Lunn. My parents spoke as if both were true, so they were.

We all have to start somewhere. This is where I emerged from. Like everyone else, my beliefs and values weren't chosen; I was born into them. With all the best intentions, my loving parents offered me a pre-packaged version of the Christian faith I had no thought of rejecting. I didn't know I could refuse it, even as I believed I couldn't reject my mum's instruction not to put my hand in the raging coal fire in the back room. This way of believing seemed to work for Mum and Dad. Invested in this particular mutation of the Christian faith, they appeared happy and fulfilled. As I inherited their DNA, I also absorbed their values and beliefs.

So, growing up, I wasn't a blank canvas onto which anything could be painted. I couldn't remain uncommitted and undecided until I got to the age when I could "make my own mind up", as some might say. Choices were made for me because of where I grew up and who I grew up with. Yes, I recognize that if I'd been born in Afghanistan, I would've almost certainly turned out as a Muslim, or in some parts of India as a Hindu, or in regions of China as . . . you get the picture.

As a potential moth, I hadn't yet realized that the whole of life is a process of emerging. There wouldn't be a magical time when I could reliably and finally make my mind up. So much of what I believed and thought would always remain provisional, tentative.

No doubt, like me, you've gone the wrong way from time to time. I've made my mind up on so many issues only to find it has made me a less pleasant version of the human being I'm supposed to be. I'd become polluted with the toxicity of my arrogance.

There were, though, things I did know, things I could be sure of without becoming cocky. For instance, that my parents loved me. I'm grateful for their love; it more than covered up the harm they and others would do to me and the damage I'd do to myself. The pre-packaged version of the faith they rooted me in (with its many gifts and deficiencies) was their attempt, in love, to offer me what they thought was the best. Despite the ever-watching God who lived at home and everywhere else, there were far more advantages than disadvantages, for, as the old book says, love covers a multitude of sins. Mum and Dad weren't perfect, but they were more than good enough.

When I reached the end of my childhood, I dangled partway out of my cocoon with some hang-ups. But I also had the distinct impression there was something greater and more mysterious than my small private existence.

Regardless of what I may have assumed over the years, I didn't arrive at my beliefs because I agreed with any theological proposition or argument. I didn't accept them because they seemed logical. I believed them because they made sense, primarily at an emotional level.

I grew up belonging to a church community held together by the glue of good, honest and upright people—upright in a nice, fluffy, but reliable way, not in a pietistic, holier-than-thou sense. Each weekend (and at odd times during the week), we'd pile into our beaten-up old Ford for the ten-minute ride to a small church squeezed onto the corner of a minor road junction in Cheadle, Cheshire, where I met adults who were wise role models. There are some I'll remember for as long as I live. They are the names we've carried in family conversations over the decades. These are the unforgettable giants and the quiet heroes of my past. If there are saints, these are better versions for me than the stone-carved figures of draughty church transepts.

Despite all the wonderfulness surrounding me, which compensated for the spookiness of my God-watched life, despite the best my parents could do to get me ready to become a full-grown moth, despite all the friends, security, nurturing and affirmation in my sometimes wacky and weird Christianity, nothing prepared me for what was to come. Nothing prepared me for what I'd face in the world beyond, once my chrysalis started to break up and fall away. Nothing prepared me for being a Christian teenager outside of family and church.

At the end of the day, we are each alone. No one else looks out through our eyes or feels what it is like to live from the inside of our bodies. Sometimes, such aloneness can feel frightening.

3

Cosseted

Before I became susceptible to insidious worry, I inhabited a charmed world, a world where the boundaries of life were aligned with the walls of our house. For my first four years, I revelled in the status of the baby of the family. Then, my younger sister, Heather, was born. She usurped my privileged position. Until then, as the youngest of three, after my brother and older sister, there was a comforting sense that I enjoyed my mother's presence in a way no one else did. Each day, Andrew and Janet went off to some unknown place: school.

I was left behind in an idyll. Being with Mum was my whole world. The cold winter days, centred on the coal fire in the back room, are well-etched in the recesses of my mind.

After trailing behind Mum each morning as she did her daily round of tasks, dinner became the pause in the day when everything turned calm, and I felt secure. In the north of England, "dinner" had never meant an evening meal. That was the alien language of our relatives from London, which still to this day feels foreign.

Dinner, at midday, might be soup and a roll, it might be a cold sandwich, it might be a hot meal. I can't remember what ours usually was. What I do remember is what followed. The open fire was poked, and extra coals were added. Then Mum would settle into her much-beloved rocking chair with her feet tucked in behind her.

As the radio mumbled with the chatter of adult voices, the one o'clock news fizzled out, and the main event (at least for me) took place: _Listen with Mother_. Whenever I hear Gabriel Fauré's _Dolly Suite_, the theme tune, I'm transported back to those far-flung days. To the heat of the fire, the creaking of the rocking chair, the strange smell of the rug on the tiled floor, smelling sweet from all that had been spilt on it and all that had been trodden into it. Lying there on the floor, running my Matchbox cars along the pattern of the carpet, a gentle voice of welcome from our large valve radio announced, "Are you sitting comfortably? Then I'll begin."

And so the adventure of story-time and songs began. I entered another place of safety.

It is never appreciated at the time, but nothing can replace such a feeling of belonging and security. I didn't know I was fortunate. I didn't realize this wasn't the experience for many who lived only a few streets from our house. I didn't know that I'd have to make sense of others' lack of maternal assurance and how their woundedness impacted them, other people and one day me.

If it also rained on the garden path beyond the French windows as my mother fell asleep, I felt all the more cossetted and connected.

With such a start, why wouldn't I accept what Mum said about God and everything else in the universe?

However, life can never always be so easy. Innocence, that lack of being wounded, should be the right of every young child in their formative years, but it never remains permanent. Some experience little of it.

I was lucky. I was fortunate. But it didn't last. It never can.

4

Aloneness

I tasted my first wounding outside our home the day I started school. Reaching my fifth birthday, I'd become a "big boy". I had to leave my fireside-cossetted life and go to school with Andrew and Janet. As it was the middle of June, most of the children in the class had already attended for many months, some for most of the school year. I was the new boy.

Clearly, the teacher hadn't anticipated my arrival when Mum dropped me off that mid-morning. As there wasn't a place ready for me, she guided me to a seat vacant because of an absent child. Then Mum left.

The boy beside me turned and said, "That's not your chair; it's Billy's." The other four children on the hexagon-shaped table all concurred with their looks of faint hostility. This was the first time I'd ever felt truly alone.

The morning didn't start well, but it soon took a bizarre turn. Another boy on our table took out his willie and peed on the floor in the middle of our six pairs of feet. We each ducked our heads under the table to watch the circle of wet as it grew bigger, expanding towards our shoes. Nothing was said. The teacher probably didn't know it had happened.

It was a lot for a young boy who'd just entered this new world by himself, alone, to take in. My life would continue to unfold in ways I never expected. Often in ways I didn't understand or know how to deal with.

When I talk about being alone, I'm not talking about loneliness but true aloneness. No one could have warned me, a child, about this distinction. Such insights must be felt and reflected upon before they can be expressed.

Being alone is one thing. Being alone and defenceless is another altogether.

Dinnertimes in primary schools have a definite order and shape to them. They have to. At my school, it started with us all going to the toilet. Then we washed our hands, after which robust dinner ladies marshalled us across the open playground, in all weathers, to a run-down Victorian hall to eat our food.

The routine always seemed to involve much queuing and waiting. I got the feeling we were a problem to these supervising adults. It was no doubt a nightmare to get a lot of young children to collect their food from the kitchen hatch and find a seat without something going awry.

The trauma I'm coming to happened on a Tuesday during the second course of the meal. I was dealt a large portion of sponge which contained a vast number of raisins. This was then covered with lashings of custard. Back at my table, I tucked into the custard and the sponge, trying to avoid the raisins. I'd never liked them.

Because I was trying to avoid the dried fruit, my progress slowed. Children who had finished left to run around and shout in the distant playground. Dinner ladies tidied up the devastation left behind. As these ladies, who appeared ancient to me, passed by my seat, they encouraged me to eat up.

After a while, seated in the far corner of the hall, I was the only child remaining. The headteacher and her staff sat talking on the stage, having finished their meal. I picked at my food and pushed it around the plate as time ticked by. After what seemed like an age, the headteacher's voice called from the stage, "Graham, come here." Surprised and ill at ease, I moved out of my seat and stood by my table, looking up the length of the hall. It seemed endless to me. I had a sinking feeling in my gut; I could easily have shat myself.

I walked the length of the hall and stood nervously in front of the stage. The voice said, "Come up here." I walked up the large central wooden steps, which had no handrail, to face the head sitting in her central commanding position. The other teachers looked on. "Graham, why won't you eat your pudding?" Was I silent, or did I speak? I can't remember. I can recall the horror of being alone and exposed in front of so many adults. I'd never experienced anything like this before, even when my mum lost her rag with me at home. I felt great shame for not liking and not eating my pudding.

I don't remember leaving the headteacher, the stage or the hall. But I can still sense the isolation, vulnerability and fear that revisited me on other occasions.

5

Faith and the mushroom cloud

They never said it, but I sensed Mum and Dad were frustrated missionaries. Like any child, I spent time lingering a few feet out of sight, listening to conversations that weren't mine. I was keen to hear if Dad might get a new car. Cars were everything to me. They were a world that made sense.

Sometimes, I heard the tail end of a row when Mum was angry with Dad in a way I thought was only reserved for us children. This wasn't a regular occurrence, but such a quarrel doesn't have to happen often to unnerve a young heart. I never got the impression our family was on the edge of collapse. More than once, though, I felt we could be on the move. Africa was mentioned: Kenya or Nigeria. I'm not sure what happened, but they never became missionary material. There was still, however, some residual rumour about Dad plying his trade in Africa as a quantity surveyor.

This came up at one of our "round-table family discussions". These functioned like small community meetings. Here, major decisions were made, such as where we might go camping in the summer. It was even more exciting to discuss who might want to redecorate their bedroom or even swap them. But yes, a move to Africa was once mooted. Dad would get a job out there, giving him and Mum a chance to get their missionary fix.

Nothing came of this. I was disappointed, especially when each day became more conflicted and unbearable as I embarked on the horror of my secondary education. I wanted a way out. I'd have gone anywhere. I wanted to be in another place. Africa sounded good to me. Later, Dad applied for a post in Hong Kong. That sounded even better. But, too bad, we stayed in the God-watched house on the south Manchester Bible Belt.

Mum and Dad were converts to Christianity. They'd recount the story of attending uniformed organizations at their local parish church in north Surrey, which, after a few years, led them to sign a pledge to follow Jesus in a Billy Graham sort of way. As "born-again" believers, they were able to answer the evangelist's question, "If you were to die tonight, do you know where you are going?" This took place within the broader context of the military stand-off between the West and the Soviet Union, with the real possibility of nuclear annihilation. Their life-changing decision to become "evangelical Christians" was most likely fuelled, in part, by fear of war. We like to think we're rational, but our choices are usually shaped by what we yearn for and fear.

The possibility of a nuclear apocalypse was a real and present dread for my parents as they married and started to raise the family. Unsurprisingly, the 2,000-year-old story from Palestine of a prophet-king was interpreted against such a pessimistic backdrop.

Had I been in their shoes, I am not sure my choices would have been any different. They'd survived the Second World War with some close scrapes. Living on the southwest corner of London alongside a major rail route to the coastal ports of Southampton, Poole and Portsmouth, their patch was fair game for the Luftwaffe's cargoes of death. Friends and acquaintances were killed, and they were scared shitless living in their blacked-out neighbourhoods night after night.

If I'd survived the Blitz, as they had, and then faced the prospect of being wiped out in a nuclear plasma blast as the Cold War unravelled, I might also have adopted Billy Graham's simplistic rhetoric of deciding whether I'd go to heaven or not when the "Russkies" dropped their nuke on me.

As Mum and Dad's belief system had been shaped by their experience and fear of war, mine was shaped second-hand by their anxieties. As a child, I can't remember a time when talk of the shooting-down of Gary Powers' spy plane over the Soviet Union, the debacle of America's failed Bay of Pigs invasion and the Cuban Missile Crisis didn't make people concerned and troubled. These weren't things anyone joked about.

Because of such talk, a chill ran down my spine whenever the air-raid siren on top of Gatley Hill House (in the park on the other side of our street) was powered up "just to check it still worked". I understood why they had to do this. But no one could tell me how I'd know if its blaring out was the warning of an incoming murderous mushroom cloud rather than a simple practice drill. I'd fed on the fear of my parents, a fear I felt in my guts whenever the right buttons were pushed.

My views were already being shaped, though I didn't realize it.

TEENAGER

6

A shocking start

I never expected to pass the eleven-plus exam to go on to the grammar school. I harboured a suspicion that a clerical error had been made in my favour. I still believe this.

Having made the grade, I expected life to take on a new trajectory marked by achievement and success. This would please Mum and Dad and reassure me I could make something of myself. Even though the validity of my entry into Burnage Grammar might've been dubious, I still expected to get a decent education. I hoped I was leaving behind what had been a mediocre performance at primary school for something better. I was relieved and proud. My parents were relieved and proud. We waited that summer through with hopeful expectation.

The hope of this new start began to ramp up the day I went with Mum to the men's outfitters in Manchester to buy my uniform. Black and white wasn't the most creative colour scheme, but it was smart to me. Once back home, there was the obligatory dress rehearsal as I showed off my kit to my admiring siblings.

The evening before my first day, I set out everything I needed with military precision and readiness: blazer, ironed white shirt, tie, cap, pencil case complete with many unnecessary accessories, satchel and well-polished shoes. The next day would be exciting, walking down the grand driveway of Burnage Grammar, maybe alongside Harry Stott, a friend of my brother, who wanted to become a journalist. What might I become?

I set off on the bus with four other new boys I didn't know. It became a dysfunctional alliance—an alliance instigated by our anxious mothers. When I got there, I didn't walk down the drive with the much-admired Harry Stott but as part of this innocent-looking fivesome. We stood out like targets on a shooting range in our pristine uniforms with neat ties and capped heads. Most boys who weren't new wore shabby and sometimes ripped jackets. They wore their ties untidily. Even though it was compulsory, none of them wore a cap.

There was no warm welcome in the playground as we had expected. It was full of grown men. Well, they looked like grown men to me. In truth, they were boys, 14- to 18-year-olds. In place of the hoped-for friendly greeting was a mood of daunting intimidation. Cap-wearing newbies were snatched from their travelling companions by these men-boys who claimed them as their "fags". They commanded them to hold their ties, for they claimed "the weight of them was bearing down too much on their necks." I ducked for cover.

Fags had to carry out menial duties and demeaning acts. Anyone in the first year was called a fag, along with a few vulnerable and young-looking boys from the second year. They were easy to spot as they wore caps and short trousers. Nothing prepared me for this. No one warned me.

The school ran on a currency of subtle and overt coercion, bullying and violence. New uniforms were ripped, caps thrown into local gardens, property damaged or stolen, books strewn across pavements and bodies bruised and beaten. The brutality was as shocking as it was fear-inducing. No one looked out to protect us. As far as I could tell, this culture of threat and cruelty was accepted as the way things were by pupils and staff alike. The message was clear: you had to "man up" and get on with it.

I mentioned nothing of this at home. Maybe I felt I should be grateful to attend such a "wonderful" establishment. I didn't think I had any right to complain.

After a few weeks, I had my first fight. It happened on the field close to the main driveway. Rosenberg had been pushing me around, and I was fit to burst. And then I did. Because I was so angry and annoyed, I flew at him in a rage. He was quite a bit bigger than me, but I was quicker. As we lunged into each other, a crowd gathered, shouting, "Fight! Fight! Fight!" Our friends egged us on with rants and expletives. It went on for what seemed like an age, and I was sure a staff member would soon turn up and march us off to see the headteacher. But none came. We became more tired. We swung our arms at each other in a frenzied, fruitless manner. Eventually, I landed a few hooks on Rosenberg's face, and he started to cry. Crying was the sign of defeat in any fight. A roar went up for me, but I was on the verge of crying too. I managed to hold back my tears, though.

Soon, the bell rang to mark the end of our lunchtime break, and we went in for registration. The word around the form room was, "Turner beat up Rosenberg!" Our form teacher, aware of the chatter, said nothing.

My success gave me a taste for violence. It established my place in the pecking order among the 120 boys of our year.

I'd won my first fight, but something was also lost. Something of my friendship with Tomlin died.

He and I had been good friends throughout our junior school years. He was witty and curious whilst also hopeless at sport. So, we were a good match. We shared interests and helped each other with our work. I'd been to his birthday parties. Significantly, Tomlin was a Jew, as was Rosenberg.

There was a close bond among the Jewish boys as they didn't attend the daily assembly where we sang from our *Christian Praise* hymn books. Their resultant solidarity turned many against them. Was I caught up in this with my anger at Rosenberg? Probably, yes.

Returning to the form room following the lunch break, triumphant but wounded, I caught a look on Tomlin's face. I knew something had changed for us. But I'd gained an appetite for fighting, which worked for me, for a while at least.

*

As my fondness for fighting developed, violence became a major issue each Saturday on the football calendar. Invariably, the weekend TV news started with images of marauding men and youths in and around the stadiums. Other European nations called it "the English disease".

Many of the adults I moved among moaned about this behaviour. "I don't know what they get out of it," they complained. But I knew. There was a buzz to violence. There was excitement. Enemies could be cowed. Everyone loved to watch a brawl. Fighting was a way to get noticed, a way to become notorious.

A few years after I left Burnage, one pupil killed another. Violence was deep in the school's psyche.

Early in my first year, I learned it wasn't wise to say I was a Christian. So, I didn't own up that I went to church each Sunday or believed in Jesus. Watts was picked on for being the most overweight boy in our class. But he was also persecuted because he was a Pentecostal Christian. It wasn't just the boys who picked on him. Some staff also singled him out, mocking him for attending Bethshan Tabernacle each week to "sing his alleluias". He bravely attempted to defend his beliefs, but, in the end, he became an atheist.

In another of the first-year classes, Bayes was also singled out. His dad was a vicar. He fought back as best he could but travelled a lonely path over the years.

At school, it was open season to pick on anyone who held religious beliefs, especially Christian ones. "Go on, show me God! See, you can't. He doesn't exist!" "The Bible is a made-up story; you can't prove it!" "What about all the other religions? Are they all going to hell, and you're not, eh?"

There was a Bible in each of our desks; it was one of our textbooks. But they were never studied; they were used for punishment. The geography teacher made efficient use of them. Making misbehaving boys stand on their chairs with their arms outstretched, he'd pile two or three Bibles on each hand, promising a worse penalty if they dropped any of them. They dropped them, of course.

A local church minister used to come in to give religious instruction. Every time he arrived, the mood was rowdy and intimidating. The class wouldn't quieten down or cooperate with him. A rumour went around his full name was Arthur Mann. One week, someone scrawled "half-a-Mann" all over the room in chalk. I felt sorry for him. Through Mum and Dad, I knew many ministers. On the whole, they were good people.

So, I decided to hide the fact I was a Christian. I wouldn't mention where I went each Sunday or anything about the small church on the minor road junction ten minutes from where we lived. Instead, I found my place in the bullying and violent culture of the playground.

My priority was to survive.

7

Compartmentalization

My days settled down uncomfortably around three centres: home, school and church. I learnt to compartmentalize my life; it became my coping strategy. At one level, it worked. But it also fuelled my nervousness.

I didn't want to be a Christian at school, and I feared others might discover I went to church. It wasn't cool to be a follower of Jesus. It wasn't safe to be a Christian. It didn't win you any friends. I was embarrassed about church and what we were supposed to believe. It affected how I behaved and made me guarded about what I said.

I did all I could to prevent the toxicity of my weekdays from polluting the other two centres. I didn't always succeed. Life tended to collapse together those bits I attempted to keep apart.

The class bully could smell fear in any boy. He was always waiting to pounce if, for instance, a memory verse from Sunday School fell out of my pocket. Then, I'd fear being derided as stupid and thick for believing in God and branded as a religious nut. This could also lead to being excluded from certain friendship groups.

It was all too easy for an unguarded conversation or an unexpected coincidence to expose my secret Christian life. Those I travelled with on the bus each morning might see me in my Sunday best as we set off for church.

One of the teachers who attended our church would sometimes acknowledge me in the corridor as we changed lessons. My friends would want to know what that was about.

Most of the time, though, nothing happened. But the fear something might was permanent and debilitating. It fed an underlying anxiety. So, I kept a low profile. There was no point in increasing my risk of exposure.

The two centres of home and church were well-connected, so much so it was hard at times to detect much of a boundary between them. On the whole, I didn't complain. I met an amazing array of people; a good number stayed over at our house.

Even before I was a teenager, I'd met people from every continent at our meal table. I'd met men who'd escaped the Biafran War in Nigeria, and one Christmas a family from Pakistan came and cooked a curry banquet for a dozen people in our kitchen long before we'd heard of chapatis. Americans turned up with weird accents, and I remember the first bottle of wine I'd ever seen in our house being a gift from German women of the Mosel Valley. Chinese students visited us along with many other fascinating people.

Looking back, I appreciate my religious framework gave me a sense of meaning and purpose. I grew up believing there was more to reality than my little world and I'm grateful for this. However, going to church each Sunday was non-negotiable and frequently dreary.

8

Church tedium

When on holiday, camping north of the border, Mum and Dad took us to a variety of churches: the Church of Scotland, the Free Church of Scotland, the Free Presbyterian Church of Scotland, and many other variations and deviations. On these visits, we four children were well-behaved. We were probably intimidated; we knew we were aliens. Although warmly greeted, we were watched. These tended to be more austere and stricter versions of the faith we knew at home; they could make God appear more frightening. We sat to sing the Psalms and stood for the prayers. The prayers were long and dreary. The sermons, always given by a man, were incomprehensible, made worse by the heavy Celtic accents of the highlands. As we drove away from each of these experiences, my parents usually said, "That was a good church." Those with longer names tended to get better reviews. It all made no sense to me. It was also not a topic to write about in the English class when term restarted in September.

Our regular Sunday jaunt while at home wasn't a great improvement on the churches in Scotland. But it was a tedium I knew. It was familiar. It was like some long-term friend you've always known, a friend you've had to rub along with.

The prayers and readings were from seventeenth-century Prayer Book texts. The hymns were about 150 years old. Many were much older. For me, as a child, it was what we did. Like anything else, if Mum and Dad did or did not do something, we children usually followed suit. There'd never been a time when I didn't consider myself a churchgoer or a Christian. In the same way, there'd never been a time when I didn't consider myself to be a Turner or a Brit.

Later in life, I had to find out who I was beyond the names, labels and tribal affiliations handed on to me by others. I had to discover *who* I truly was. I had to explore the most important question of life: who on earth am I?

It wasn't a conscious process, but family and faith planted in me three core values. I should try to do what is right. I should seek to live out my faith each day. I shouldn't disappoint my parents.

These were easier said than done. I discovered they were impossible much of the time. So, I did other things to create excitement.

9

Vandalism

I've never had difficulty finding fun. I haven't suffered from feeling low or depressed except for a few brief moments of self-pity as a teenager.

So many things are hilarious. Many other things have the potential to be funny. And there are those things that shouldn't be laughed at yet are still amusing. Laughing has got me out of a lot of trouble, and into some too.

Dad was a practical joker. He taught me how to tease people. There was a lot of humour and laughter at home; teasing each other was a part of family life. However, teasing is double-edged. Joking is often at the expense of someone else. It can serve to weaken familial ties as well as strengthen them. Both happened at home.

I earned myself a privileged place within the family as the joker. I've never found it hard to make people smile and even laugh, not in a stand-up comedic way but in those usual interactions of each day. Making people laugh has many benefits. During lessons at school, it broke the life-sapping monotony. Nothing was better than mucking about in a practical class such as chemistry, woodwork, or out on the sports field. It also won me friends. Only a few boys thought messing around was a waste of time.

At home, I got out of all sorts of trouble through humour. If Mum or Dad told me off (and it wasn't too serious), I'd do all I could to make them laugh, defuse the matter, and escape any punishment. I can still hear Dad's words, "Stop it, Graham! I'm trying to tell you off." In our marriage, I know I've wheedled my way out of trouble with R on more than one occasion using the same tactic. I've used the technique at difficult parish meetings, sometimes to defuse a tricky conflict or even to help me get my own way. I have to admit the technique can at times be construed as manipulation. On the whole, people have liked me for it. But, as I got older, I recognized more of its dark side.

Such darkness also gave me a taste for vandalism. Many look down on those who fight as if they themselves have no feelings of aggression. They regard those who smash up property with the same attitude. But who doesn't like to hear the smashing of unwanted glass ornaments and other household items as they are thrown into the skip? Who doesn't feel a thrill in taking a sledgehammer to an old garden shed or outbuilding that has served its time? All that's different is that vandals damage property which isn't theirs, but the buzz is the same.

While Andrew and I fought like ferrets in a sack, we were close as brothers in a chalk-and-cheese sort of way. Life was always harder for him than for me within and beyond the family. But from an early age, he showed me the excitement of breaking minor rules and gave me the courage to become daring.

While on our holidays in Scotland, we'd spend hours exploring by ourselves, often going where we shouldn't. One day, we found ourselves on a railway line where we threw stones and kicked around old pieces of junk. Trains only came along the line every couple of hours, so we felt safe. After 20 minutes or so, we came across a station that was deserted. Walking onto the platform, we peered into the empty, locked waiting room and ticket office. Then, all of a sudden, Andrew picked up a stone and threw it straight through the window of the waiting room. The silence of the station was broken by the smashing and falling of glass. I couldn't believe what he'd done. He couldn't believe what he'd done. So, thinking if it was good enough for him, then it was good enough for me, I heaved a rock across the tracks to smash the window of the ticket office opposite. In a heightened frenzy, we couldn't stop laughing. We put in more windows until we ran out of ammunition. Full of fear and excitement, we sped along the platform, escaping the scene of the crime. Running up onto the road bridge, we surveyed our work with a sense of amazed achievement. From there, we attempted to finish the windows we'd missed, but with limited success.

I understand vandals as I understand men who fight. I don't condone either; their actions have serious consequences, sometimes tragic. But I know where such energy comes from and why it is contagious. When things aren't going well, it is natural to look for other ways to let off steam.

How did I square this violence against people and property with my faith's ingrained principle that we should always do what is right? I couldn't. But by this time, my three centres were starting to spin out of control. I could've easily entered a self-destructive downward spiral. I found no link between the church-promoted diet of faith I received each Sunday and the hellish reality I survived during the week. Preachers instructed me to tell boys at school about Jesus. But no one knew or tried to find out what my week was like. Church became my alternative reality, which only made sense within its own activities or remit.

My life as a teenager followed a predictable and worrying pattern. Then, a shock knocked me sideways and shook me to the core.

1 0

Alistair

When we reached the top of Sunday School, we moved on to the afternoon Bible class, bearing the strange name Covenanters. We were all given a small metal badge in the shape of a medieval crusader's shield to wear. The class for boys was half a mile down the road from the girls.

Each Sunday afternoon, we gathered in a dark, dank room at the back of the large rectory. Well-meaning adults spent time painting the room in weird colours. They furnished it with their old sofas. In the corner was a piano painted white. To make it sound trendy, someone had pushed drawing pins into its hammers. It sounded like an out-of-tune, dysfunctional harpsichord.

The weekly pattern was predictable. About 20 of us turned up for the meetings. We mumbled Christian songs to tunes such as the Beatles' *Yellow Submarine*. There were prayers, readings and quizzes. The main feature was supposed to be the Bible study. These studies were mind-numbingly dull; nothing in them addressed the issues I faced each week at Burnage.

Apart from piling up smashed pieces of furniture on top of each other before the class started, the quiz was the only other highlight or hint of excitement of those afternoons. Most of the boys came from homes where faith was taken less seriously. There was one exception to this: Alistair. Like me, he was recognized as coming from a "keen" Christian family.

We were close friends, but when it came to the quiz, we were rivals. As we had far more Bible knowledge than the rest of the group, we were always placed on opposing teams. I guess keeping us apart kept the thrill of the quiz alive for the leaders.

The shock happened the Sunday Alistair failed to turn up. We were all ready to start. I sat on a wooden chair perched on top of a well-wrecked sofa at the back of the room. Aware of some murmuring among the leaders, I asked where Alistair was. The reply was simple and brief, "Oh, he died during the week." Nothing more was said. Soon, the *Yellow Submarine* started up, and the meeting got underway. It was as if it was any other Sunday afternoon. Alistair was never mentioned again. I was stunned. At the end of the class, I cycled the two miles home to tell my parents the news. After a few phone calls, they confirmed it was true. Alistair had died of a congenital heart condition during the week.

I'm somewhat comforted that if anything like this happened today, it would be handled differently. The emotional intelligence of society and its institutions has come on in leaps and bounds. Even so, it was poorly managed, and this was no comfort to a 13-year-old boy who'd lost a good friend, his only Christian friend.

I spent the next week roaming around inside my head trying to make sense of it. It felt more like shock than grief, but the one does envelop the other. I'd never suffered a death before. All my grandparents were alive and healthy. Even our old cat, Noddy, was still going strong. What was grief supposed to feel like? What was I supposed to do? I didn't know. I know I didn't cry. Did I ever grieve?

The biggest impact Alistair's death made on me was to place Billy Graham's strapline centre stage. "If you were to die tonight, do you know where you are going?" Maybe Alistair knew; he looked like he knew, although we never talked about it. Then the horror hit me. Maybe Alistair is watching me much like the UNSEEN GUEST. If so, he'd see how I lived my life of sin: violence, hypocrisy, lust and denial. I was aghast. I promised myself I'd do better, promised God I'd do better, and promised Alistair I'd do better. But deep down, I knew I didn't have the strength, the courage or the ability to do any better. While his death increased my inner turmoil and my burden of grief, I also had a strange sense of a presence with me—a kindly presence.

For good and not-so-good reasons, Alistair's death helped me lean in towards this Jesus I'd been told about almost every day. While my distress at school deepened, there was a stirring within me that felt okay, even good. While losing my friend troubled me, it also made me more aware. Even though it waxed and waned, the new sense of presence remained with me. Because of what happened that fateful Sunday, I knew something I'd never known before. It wasn't anything I could put into words. To use religious language, it was, I believe, what some might call an experience of "God".

1 1

The school's dysfunction

When I was 14, I hit a new academic low. I received a disastrous mark for an end-of-term exam: 4 per cent. My teacher's comment in my report stated, "Hopeless case (for history)." My only consolation was I didn't come at the bottom of the class. Twenty-five years later, I was diagnosed with dyslexia. With all this going on, I started to develop a stammer.

I guess Mum and Dad worried about me. Most parents worry about their children. They had probably hoped getting me into the grammar school would be the making of me. They didn't know what was going on. We had no shared language that enabled them to discover it.

The school merged with another to become the largest all-boys comprehensive in Britain. This only added to its decline and disintegration.

Decades later, soon after I became the rector of Macclesfield, the local community orchestra and choir held a concert at my church. I attended and gave the welcome, introducing myself. Various folk came and said hello during the interval. A man in his seventies approached me and said, "Do you know who I am?" I knew immediately who he was from 40 years before; I even remembered his name. He taught me music for my first two years at Burnage High. He was undoubtedly surprised, even disbelieving, that someone like me was holding such a responsible job. I confessed to him that the school hadn't done me much good. He responded by telling me he hadn't fared well either. He'd been forced to take early retirement because of the impact stress had on his health.

The school's dysfunction created many victims. His wellbeing suffered, and I was compelled to hide my faith.

1 2

The sticker incident

I wasn't comfortable living with my hypocrisy and my schizophrenic lifestyle. I wasn't at ease with myself. But I didn't feel I could do anything to alleviate the disconnect. I could sometimes avoid it for a while when there was enough distraction, but I could never escape it properly.

When I was 16, the few threads by which I hung onto my delicate personal integrity almost snapped. A visiting gospel preacher from America turned up. Arthur Blessitt was carrying a wooden cross around the world. Three or four hundred young people filled a local church when he visited. I was there, hopeful this might help me become an effective Christian. Blessitt was a preacher on Sunset Strip, Hollywood. The Strip was known for its nightlife, clubs and bars, and as a base for many musicians and bands. He was applauded for preaching the gospel of Jesus in a place regarded as a cesspit of debauchery and sin. But Sunset Strip sounded like a place of interest and colour to me, not all bad. I was intrigued. I would've liked to have visited Hollywood.

The preacher came with a gospel band, who sang *He's got the whole world in his hands*. Then, after 20 minutes of loud preaching, the larger-than-life Blessitt told us we must go out and tell our friends about Jesus. He gave us strips of Jesus stickers. In the excitement of the moment, we grabbed them as if our lives depended on them. "If you don't know how to start a conversation about Jesus with your friends tomorrow," Blessitt said, "take one of these 'Jesus loves you' stickers and place it on the end of your nose. It'll get people talking." I thought it'd get me killed! But such was the force of the man's personality and tone we all felt we should take a clear stand for Jesus. I thought, "I must do this." I left the meeting with a dozen stickers and a silent promise to "do the right thing for Jesus".

The following morning, I sat around a large table with six classmates in our form room. In my blazer pocket, three stickers weighed heavily on my spirit. I thought, this is the moment; we're all sitting here waiting for the register to be taken. So I peeled a sticker off its glossy backing paper. It was on my index finger, under the table, ready to be placed on the end of my nose. I paused. I couldn't do it. I didn't have the courage. I didn't have the balls to do this one simple thing. My failure to be a good Christian was compounded. I felt deflated and a bit relieved, but also guilty.

I felt the same guilt when listening to our vicar preach at church. In one sermon, he spoke about the final judgement at the end of the world. He asked us to imagine the whole of humanity standing before the throne of God. As Christians, we were destined for heaven, of course, so we were stood to one side. Then he asked us to imagine looking across everyone gathered. What would we feel if we saw someone we knew who wasn't going to heaven? What would it be like if we'd never told them about Jesus? What if they looked us in the eye with disappointment and said, "But you never told me"?

This sort of thing made me think about my grandpa who was adamant he wasn't a Christian. If he went to hell when he died, how would heaven ever be good if I knew he was in eternal punishment? Nobody could give me a convincing answer, especially my mum, who I guessed was also worried about her father.

I thought about the husband of a woman at our church. He was a brilliant trumpeter who played in a jazz band late on Saturday nights. Because of this, he'd have a lie-in on Sunday mornings and miss the church service. He was, therefore, labelled a non-Christian. It was all harsh and black and white.

*

When I finished my fifth year at school, my troubles worsened. The important GCE O-level exam results were published during the summer holidays. As no staff were in school over the summer break, the results were taped to the inside of the office window for all to see.

I felt anxious as Mum drove me to school. Thankfully, when we arrived, no one else was there. We pulled up by the office window, and I jumped out of the car. Scanning my eye down the list of names confirmed my worst fears—I had failed all my exams. Mum simply said, "Come on, get back in the car." We drove home in silence. I'd failed my education.

As I hadn't told my friends about Jesus, I'd also failed as a Christian. I hadn't read my Bible or prayed every day. I was embarrassed about the church and Christianity. But I didn't want to let go of this Jesus who seemed to me to be the real deal. I also didn't want to lose what I'd gained through the pain following Alistair's death. I was between a rock and a hard place with nowhere to go. I blamed myself and lived alone with my sense of guilt and shame. I told no one.

1 3

Remedial

Before things got better, they got worse.

Following my spectacular examination failure, I returned to the deep, dark hell of school with a heavy heart. I was in my sixth year. But I wasn't in the sixth form as I had to repeat my fifth year. We were in the "remedial year".

Seven of us returned to a school that had failed us once for it to fail us yet again. We were a symptom and constant reminder of the school's dysfunction. Defeated and disgraced, we haunted the school's corridors, invisible to anyone looking for success or potential. We sat mutely at the back of classes of boys a year younger than us. They were like a different generation. Teachers either ignored us or picked on us. Nobody seemed concerned to find out why our performance had been so poor. It was our fault and our fault alone. I started to believe this.

Would anything ever become of me? I tried not to think about it. Was this denial or despair? I've no idea. Life became a matter of living one day at a time, but not in the spirit of the old Country and Western song sung to *Sweet Jesus*. Oh yes, I still believed, but little about faith was sweet to me. I was trying to survive the ignominy of school as best I could. Humour, where it could be found, and the hope of the four o'clock home-time bell, kept me going.

Atheism was an attractive option as no one answered my prayers—no one in the heaven above nor on the earth below. There was no peace dividend from following Jesus. I was imprisoned in a desperate place, seemingly of my own making. No light shone in this place that I could see. It felt like nobody was looking out for me; no one was covering my back. Even a love I'd hoped for slipped from my grasp. She was never going to win my parents' approval, for she was from a "broken home". Damaged goods. Not good enough for me. But I wasn't good enough for me either.

I would have become an atheist but for the fact I couldn't un-experience what I'd already encountered. I couldn't un-know what I'd sensed after

Alistair's death. Even "agnostic" wasn't enough to contain what I was and where I stood. I had an inherited faith, a traditional faith, a faith consisting of a jumble of words, ideas and images, which I fought to make sense of. I attempted to learn by rote, to memorize what I thought I was supposed to believe. At best, this would only ever be second-hand. But deep within me, I'd sensed something, an experience, a love, a knowing I couldn't shake off. The hand-me-down Christianity I lived in became a problem for me as it didn't fit with my positive experiences of presence I'd known, nor with my apparently godless weekdays.

I held it all together in silence.

STUDENT

1 4

A ray of hope

I completed my remedial year of shame, scraping through with three poor passes.

Then, my father surprised me by enrolling me on an A-level course at the further education college a half-an-hour bike ride away. Was this a demonstration of his trust in me or an act of desperation on his part? I don't know how he made his decision, but it was the best thing that could have happened to me.

For the first time in six years, those who taught me called me by my first name and treated all students with respect. The college buildings were light, clean and airy. The lecturers believed in their subjects with a contagious passion. Never before had I known such a positive educational experience. It felt like a new day had dawned. I hoped to do well, and I did.

While I hoped I'd shake off the shame and failure of my past, college would also be where I'd realize my struggle with the surveillance God had not been left behind.

On my first day at college, all new students gathered in the main hall. No doubt we were all apprehensive about how the day would unfold. I sat on a chair and looked around at all these people I didn't yet know. I was startled when I saw someone who, I found out later, was called James. He looked friendly and smiled as he gazed around the room. That was fine. What wasn't fine was the large sticker on his left lapel for all to see: "Jesus loves you." I felt a panic rush through me and I avoided eye contact. I hoped he'd be on a different course—maybe on an apprenticeship or training as a police cadet. So, the enjoyment of this new beginning was tainted by a smiling face and a Jesus sticker.

As it turned out, James would be in my part of the college but not taking any of the same courses. In time, I would bump into him, it couldn't be avoided. It seemed there was nowhere to hide, no escape from my embarrassment. James compounded my problems. He did what I failed to do. He wasn't ashamed to stand up for Jesus, whereas I was.

He was the witness so many preachers implored us to be. I wasn't. He behaved as we were supposed to behave. He even wore a sticker. Was I doomed never to escape my predicament? Would my shame always stalk me?

A couple of months into my first term, Dad surprised me again. He accepted a new job in Aberdeen. I knew the city was somewhere in Scotland, but nothing more. I had no idea it was 350 miles away. My elder sister and I were to remain behind. I lodged with an elderly widow around the corner from our church. Excited by my new independence as a 17-year-old, I wondered if this might be my undoing. There would now be no one in my new home to check up on me or enquire what I had been up to. I was aware there was a danger in my newfound freedom.

1 5

Independence

Experiencing educational success after so many years of failure was more than wonderful. Over all the years, I'd never come in the top half of any class. Now, I even came top at times. I loved the learning; there was a buzz to it. It was hard to believe I was living the same life. It was hard to believe I was the same person.

Others talked about leaving home, I could boast that home had left me. In my freedom, I enjoyed some firsts. I stayed up late into the night watching films on Mrs Farley's black and white television. At home, we'd never had a telly. I was raised on a diet of Radio 4 documentaries and dramas, and *Saturday Night is Music Night* on Radio 2. Now, I was feasting on spaghetti westerns and Second World War films. I was hooked and there was lost time to make up.

A few weeks after I started college, there was a bomb hoax. No doubt some disgruntled student wanted to avoid his class. The lads I was with decamped down to the pub. I'd never been in a pub before. I was a beer virgin. A condemning mantra hung over us as church young people: "If Jesus came back tonight, would you want him to find you sitting in a pub drinking beer?" Jesus never came back that day, and I lost my beer virginity. Much later, I learned the man from ancient Palestine would have been sitting in the pub already waiting for us to arrive.

Not long after this, three guys from my church took me on my first pub crawl. For some reason, they didn't have the same hang-ups. The four of us drank four pints in four pubs in two hours. This was a lot for a boy who'd only ever consumed half a pint of bitter. I remember running down the centre of the road, shouting and laughing out loud on our way to the last pub. I also remember returning to Ian's house, where his dad eyed us up. He was kind. He didn't say anything and I didn't feel well the next day.

My mother, probably worried about having left me behind, paid for me to have driving lessons. I passed my driving test in a blue Ford Escort. Life was good and life was sweet.

In time, I realized I knew two other students at the college. Twins Sarah and Julie were taking a secretarial course. Their father was a friend of Dad's through the building trade and via the local church network. We'd seen each other at events across crowded halls, but they were shy and we never spoke. I was reticent when I saw them at college. They were from an even more serious Christian background than mine.

I'd pass them on the campus with their long, flowing blonde hair. They were identical, although I could tell the difference. We'd nod and say hello as we passed, but nothing more. They were attractive girls, but I never saw either as a potential girlfriend. There is an assumption that men are always attracted to blonde women. But this isn't always true. The old film title *Gentlemen Prefer Blondes* is wrong. For me, the dark-headed woman has always appeared more alluring.

Sarah and Julie may never have been a romantic possibility, but they were a threat. They were aware I was a Christian and no doubt expected me to attend the college's Christian Union. I guessed they'd let James know about me. As Christian young people, we knew what was expected of us. Because of this, they posed a risk of blowing my cover with my classmates. I was powerless to control the danger they posed.

One lunchtime, I gave my friends the slip and made my way down to the weekly meeting of Christians. Just over a dozen students sat in a semi-circle. The twins smiled because I'd come, but then they averted their eyes. James nodded towards me and started the meeting. I can't remember much about it, but I can remember what it made me feel: awkward and ill at ease. The atmosphere was stilted and far from relaxed, so I was sure I wasn't the only one feeling out of sorts. I didn't want my friends to see me there, so I never went again.

What was happening to me? Whenever I was out of church circles, anything to do with Christianity sent me into a tailspin. It was as if it provoked an allergic reaction, but I didn't want to be like this. I believed in Jesus. Something impacted me in a way I couldn't deny. Yet, I lived with a dissonance I couldn't resolve.

I completed my two years at college with, for me, some outstanding exam results. I was happy and proud, my parents were delighted—and surprised.

Then, I was to move to another city. Maybe there I'd start to live properly for Jesus?

1 6

University

I never expected to go to university. Aged 19, I was independent of home; everything was up to me. I now made my own choices. With a university grant, I also had financial independence.

Crossing the Pennines to start a new life studying engineering at Bradford University was an important transition for me. The university allocated me a shared room.

I arrived at the halls of residence before my roommate. It wasn't long, though, before Bernard arrived. We chatted and then proceeded to unpack. As we shuffled around each other, putting our belongings into cupboards and onto shelves, I felt this sense of urgency. I must come clean. I must be courageous and say who I am. I mustn't continue hiding. I blurted out, "I'm sorry, but I am a Christian." There, it was done! It was out in the open. Bernard's reply was as simple as it was disarming. "It's okay; it isn't a crime, you know."

We easily succumb to self-doubt. Had I made too much of coming out to my friends? Or did other believers find it easier to inhabit the two worlds of Christian and non-Christian? Was I weaker or more ineffective than others? It often felt I held onto faith with one hand while batting it away with the other.

In those days, engineering was an even more male-dominated discipline than it is today. Of the intake of 60 on our course, only one was a woman. All the lecturers were male. The masculine culture was nowhere near as brutal as my school's hostile environment, but still, it didn't feel hospitable to religious conviction or God. My small circle of friends on the course were aware of my faith, but they rarely mentioned it. I sensed they thought it was a bit of a nerdy interest.

I threw in my lot with the Christians on campus. This meant I spent less time with my course mates. I slipped into religious activities more easily than I wanted to. But I was anxious to keep my faith and didn't trust my ability to hold on to it if I became too involved with others.

The Christian scene was also exciting. I'd never been among so many people of a similar age who believed the same as me. This was no small church on the corner of a minor road on the south side of Manchester. I didn't feel like a despised minority. Many other people valued what I thought was important. And there were girls, lots of them.

Rooms in halls of residence were only available for the first year. So, during my second year, I moved into a large house with some other lads. It soon became known as "Toller" as it was near the top of Toller Lane.

During our university years, it became the glue that held many of us together. It prevented us from going off on mad benders. We were all believers, although from different traditions and persuasions.

Soon, Toller became something more than student accommodation. It took on the feeling of a home. It wasn't just where we lived; it was where we belonged. We weren't just a bunch of students living together; we became brothers. We lived like a family with shared joys and sorrows, duties and experiences. It became a place of safety, even when we fell out.

Over the four decades since those student days, we've maintained our sense of family, sticky with nostalgia. We spend a weekend together every other year. We've grown in different ways, sometimes on diverging paths. Like any family, we've had to negotiate what we find uncomfortable and what we disagree about, including matters of belief. But it feels like we are tied together with something thicker than blood.

Our bond has held us and helped us get to where we are today with our rejoicings and sadnesses. This bond feels like it is made of the same stuff I sensed when Alistair died. Some may want to express this in religious language, but it is more profound for me than that. Like any true love, it cannot be spoken.

1 7

Factory

When I crossed the Pennine Hills to start at university, I knew I was starting a new life. I entered an unknown world when I left behind the familiarities, friends and experiences of Manchester. I didn't know anybody who'd been to university. This was to be a make-or-break moment for me. Would I live a hundred per cent as a Christian? Would I fulfil the expectations of my parents and my elders that, consciously and unconsciously, travelled with me? But I had to learn that life is never straightforward or simple. None of us does anything a hundred per cent. We all operate in the shadowy arena of mixed motives and uncertain principles. My doubts and ambiguities were always close at hand.

My blurted-out apology to Bernard may have made it clear to him that I was one of these believer types, but it didn't exorcise my dis-ease at having a faith and a God. Working in a factory as part of my course also brought this home to me.

I chose to spend my six-month industrial placements at an aircraft factory in Cheshire. As a child, I'd spent many days plane-spotting at Ringway Airport and my evenings making model aeroplanes. So, I looked forward to my apprenticeship at the place where real planes were made.

The business of plane-making is quite different today. Now, the factories are spotlessly clean. Where I went to work was dirty and noisy. Only men worked on the shop floor. The few women there staffed the admin offices.

As I entered the works with the other newbies, I recalled my first day at secondary school. While different, it was still abusive, crude and exploitative. It was a grown-up version of the school playground where few seemed to be grown up.

At school, I'd seen the odd (mild) dirty magazine our form teacher passed around. In the factory, every fitter's tool cabinet was his shrine to sexploitation. On the outside, they were adorned with a class of porn I'd never seen before. But when opened up, the pictures pinned inside these lockers were truly graphic and shocking. My fellow apprentices were divided. Some laughed and guffawed while others were dismayed, for they, too, had sisters. I'm no saint. I had looked at stuff that exploited women and material which wasn't good for me. But this was at another level. The bravado and macho culture of the factory exploited women and was abusive towards anyone who exhibited any weakness or difference.

This wasn't the place to engage in religious talk or try to win a convert as the Jesus-hippie Blessitt said I should. This was no place for a Jesus sticker.

A lad a few years older than me worked as an apprentice in the photographic department. He came from the local church I'd started to attend. We rarely spoke about church while at work, nor did we speak about work while at church. It was never voiced; we worried about blowing each other's cover. I could see in his eyes what I felt in my guts—fear.

The man who ran the works' Christian Union was small and walked with a severe limp. He was an outsider in the factory in more ways than one. But he was courageous.

Despite this oppressive atmosphere, I met some wonderful people. While playing cards over lunchtime, some could make you laugh until you wept and your sides hurt. I came across men who took the time to show me interesting things about how the aircraft worked. Somebody asked if I'd ever listened to Rachmaninov's *Second Piano Concerto*. I'd never heard of Rachmaninov until then. We'd go to the pub on a Friday lunchtime to chortle and tell stories. Then, we'd return to work and, surprisingly, we weren't as good at drilling straight holes in sheet aluminium as we were in the morning.

There were plenty of men I liked to be around. But they were often dismissive and rude about anything concerning belief or religion. I sometimes felt empathy with them, even a sense of camaraderie. This often placed me on the wrong side of the faith/no faith line. I wondered if I was spending too much time on the wrong side. But that sense of companionship, often found when men worked well together, felt good and seemed healthy.

The church I attended during my spells in industry was earnest. At a human level, it was flourishing. I made friends in the large youth group, but I knew I was passing through. There were many bright and engaging girls whose company I enjoyed. However, there were never any I fancied for anything more serious.

It was at this church that I met a woman who changed the way I thought. She was much older than me.

1 8

Feminism

Through the church's youth group, I made a friend in Chas. Reflecting the congregation's earnestness, he and I decided to meet once a week to pray together. We wanted to be serious about our shared faith. This arrangement benefited me because I'd stay on for the family's evening meal. His parents were excellent cooks; the food was always amazing. They were also interesting people, especially his mother. It was because of her that I decided to become a feminist.

One evening, as we sat around their meal table, she told us she was due to read the Bible passage at the coming Sunday service: "Wives, submit to your husbands as to the Lord. For the husband is the head of the wife as Christ is the head of the church." As Chas and I tried to be good Bible-believing boys, she challenged us, "Do you think this is the word of God for all time?" We attempted to put up a defence. Our simplistic argument, based on our Sunday School understanding of the Bible, was that it must be right because it was in scripture. I cannot exactly remember how she responded that evening, but what she said challenged and changed me.

A quirk of circumstances reinforced her argument about the roles of men and women. Many domestic roles in their home were reversed from what was typical in those days. Much of this was down to her having a prosthetic limb. Chas called it her wooden leg. Because of her disability, his dad did all the laundry as she couldn't bend down to reach into the washing machine. Then, because she had to drive to work, the controls on their car were adapted to suit her. She was, then, the driver of the family. Many of their domestic arrangements were the complete opposite of my parents', on the face of it, because of her disability.

Chas' mum showed me how the church had devalued women, controlled many aspects of what they did and prevented them from living fulfilled lives. She argued that the church, with its male clergy, used parts of the Bible to defend the status quo. Even though I'd been nurtured in the old (male-dominated) way of thinking, she convinced me otherwise. This was a new way of thinking. I was a convert. From here, I started to wonder if my present-day context might have an important part to play in helping me to interpret the Bible. I was still unsure, however.

As a man, and a white man at that, it wasn't always easy to see how the world and the church had been rigged in my favour. I'd baulked at the feminist strapline "Women are people too." I didn't get it. But that day, I discovered that self-emptying is necessary for the journey.

A long time has passed since I sat at their table of hospitality and started to learn this lesson. If I am a feminist, I'm not much of a feminist yet. The world is often still orientated for the benefit of people like me, even those of us embarrassed about our religious beliefs.

After each placement at the factory, I returned to university carrying my luggage and the heavy load of my unease. Our Toller home had become a sanctuary, though, where we talked and argued about many things as a band of brothers. But some deeper concerns weren't discussed. In hindsight, I wonder whether this was because we weren't ready to divulge much weightier matters. We'd all grown up with various religious assumptions. Our lack of maturity prevented us from having the courage to voice the darkness we harboured. Maybe we didn't have the maturity or insight to understand what was happening within us.

1 9

Mission

During my third year at university, the Christian Union decided to hold a mission. It was a week-long programme of events to share our beliefs with the hope a few new folk could be drawn in. I ended up on the planning committee. I didn't want to do this, but it was something I thought I ought to do if I was serious about what I believed. For good or for ill, a sense of duty propelled me. Two events from that week are etched in my memory—for all the wrong reasons.

The planning committee decided a literature stall should be set up in the main bar each lunchtime. Books and publications were made available for students and staff to take. Positioned inside the entrance, everyone coming in for lunch could see it. All the committee members and a few volunteers were allotted a day to be on duty. Even though I was horrified at the thought of parading my faith so publicly, I turned up to do my allotted 90-minute slot. After all, this is what you did if you followed Jesus. Such messages had been embedded into my consciousness over the years. They coerced and intimidated me into doing what I didn't always want to do. "Remember all Jesus has done for you. Is it such a great thing for you to do this for him?" "Jesus died for every man, woman and child on the planet; won't you tell them about this?" This pressure of guilt was forever an undercurrent.

I dreaded seeing my course mates that day as they crashed through the doors for their lunchtime pint. Many would've been surprised to find me among the God squad. I feared losing their respect. I feared being misunderstood. I feared being associated with a mindset I was already uncomfortable with. I feared many things.

If only I could find some way to tell them what I'd sensed and felt through life's ups and downs. But I didn't have a way to voice it without all the crass assumptions they had about Christians flagging up in their minds. Was I an oddball? On the one hand, I was part of a great religious tradition that stretched back into Jewish heritage. But I also felt like a misfit and a failure. I was uncomfortable with how we portrayed our faith during the mission week. But I wasn't sure how we could do it better as I hadn't learnt how to be honest.

It was significant that the volunteers scheduled to be with me on the stall that day either didn't turn up, turned up late or left early. They all came with excuses, of course. I guessed what was going on inside them. They were a little different to me. I was resentful. As a committee member, I was expected to be there for the full 90 minutes. I was left holding the baby. If only it was just a baby.

The other event was held on the Friday evening. It also riled me. The large dance floor alongside the bar where we'd held our literature stand was booked. A band was arranged, and a lively speaker. We had a massive push at our weekly meetings to get members to bring friends along. Being on the committee, I was part of this push. If I was part of the push, the least I could do was invite someone along. I didn't place a Jesus sticker on my nose when I turned up for lectures, but I did try to ask Brian to come along. It was a weak effort. I got on well with him. He knew I hung out with the Christians on campus. He and I worked on experiments which formed part of our engineering course. Together, we'd work out the "fiddle factor" required to ensure our results turned out correctly. If anyone was safe to invite, it was Brian. If anyone was to be forgiving of the madness I was involved in, it was Brian. So I asked him to come. He said he'd try.

On the day, I helped set up the venue. Once we were ready, we waited. Not far from the dance floor, the bar heaved with students starting their weekend with a wild evening out. A few folk turned up I didn't recognize. To save face with my Christian friends, I hoped Brian would turn up. To save face with my non-Christian friends, I hoped he wouldn't. I also feared Tony from Preston might see me if he came to the bar. Tony was on a different course to me, but he spent time in industry on the same placement, at the factory where I hadn't been honest about what I did on Sundays. Tony was a big talker and loved to take the piss. Word would undoubtedly get out if he saw me.

The large dance floor was about the size of a tennis court. The musicians with their PA looked small, tucked away at the far end. Various team members who'd come with the visiting speaker mingled with us as we watched the clock.

Then, the band got underway. They were okay. They were competent and attempted to knock out a broad range of music. I didn't recognize much of it, however. The speaker did a valiant job. I say valiant, as not many people turned up. The dance floor's enormous size made the event look poorly attended. After a couple of hours, we finished off and escaped back home.

My job was done. I was relieved Brian didn't come. I'm convinced it wouldn't have been a game-changer for him. My ongoing friendship with him was far more important to me. We met up again on Monday morning. Nothing was said about the event. I returned to life as usual; it was as if I'd never been on a mission committee.

Something was wrong with me, but suddenly I didn't care, for I met a girl. I had found love.

2 0

The orbit of love

I'd first spotted R early on, soon after starting university. One evening in our halls, I sat on the window ledge of a crowded room. There was plenty of conversation and chatter. Then, two girls crept into the room and sat on the floor, almost under the table. I noticed them, and particularly I noticed R. It wasn't long before we became part of the same circle of friends as we attended the same church on Sundays.

University was a wonderful new experience for me. I made so many new friends. It was enjoyable to be among girls. It was good to be near R. We grew closer together in a stop/start sort of way. Sometimes, it felt like a relationship was going to happen. Sometimes, it felt like it never would.

We were like planets of similar momentums orbiting around each other in a wobbly, erratic fashion. We had to learn to find the love which drew and dragged us together.

There was little rationale to this. It was too delightful and she was too delightful. The volatile fuel of lust and desire spelt risk and excitement along with enchantment and companionship.

The romance that kick-starts any relationship is, as we all know, never all unbounded joy and happiness. It also has to be a learning process. The coming together of two colliding planets is a messy business, and the outcome uncertain. Nothing is guaranteed. Breaking and losing, together with finding and bonding, have to happen if there is going to be any degree of a long-lasting relationship within which delight is to reside.

I had to learn what it meant to fall into R's orbit. My love had to be stretched beyond the romantic notions necessary to get us started. I had to learn that falling in love needed to be accompanied by a measure of vulnerable engagement. Love always comes at a price.

R did satisfy a critical requirement. She had a bob of dark hair, thick and healthy. She claimed I married her for her money, but it isn't true; I married her for her hair.

The hippie preacher from Sunset Strip berated us many years earlier for not telling our friends about Jesus. When we fall in love, he said, we go around telling everyone about it; we can't restrain ourselves. So, he continued, if we do this because of a girl or boy, how much more should we do this for Jesus?

When I saw R and fell in love after an erratic early romance, I didn't go around telling everyone. I was coy about it. The news only got out after a housemate, Jeff, spotted us walking arm-in-arm around town late into the night. Some things are too precious and delicate to spread around as if they are media fodder. We were still exploring and uncertain in our new love.

Maybe I didn't talk much about Jesus to all and sundry because of the same tentative explorings and uncertainties. I knew something, but I didn't know how well I knew it.

2 1

In-laws

Introducing your special one to parents is usually accompanied by anxiety. We travelled the seven-hour train journey up the east coast to the Granite City of Aberdeen. While I was driven more by passion in pursuing R than any objective criteria, Mum and Dad would major on objective criteria. Would R meet their expectations? Would they think we were well-suited? I was aware she didn't meet some.

My family stood in the tradition of being a Bible-believing family. To use insider jargon, we were "conservative evangelicals" (nothing, or at least little, to do with the Tories). R wasn't. While from a decent church-going folk, her family were considered "middle-of-the-road Christians". It looks terrible when these words are committed to paper, but in those days conservative evangelical Christians looked down on middle-of-the-road Christians, judging them as wishy-washy. Disagreements among Christians have been destructive and shameful. I'd reason to be anxious.

For me, R's difference was intriguing. While I still paraded my conservative evangelical arrogance, her otherness drew me to her. Always on the hunt for facts, information and opinions, I wanted to know how and why others saw life differently. It seemed that knowing this could only make me a better person. There wasn't any good reason not to understand why other people were different from me, even if they were wrong (which they would've been, of course).

The visit was going well. R's gentleness, humour and warmth eased our passage into those few days. Mum and Dad were charmed. I started to feel sure she'd be accepted.

Then, one lunchtime, a meat was served that R had never seen on her plate before (or since): boiled lamb's heart. Each piece was large, still clearly heart-shaped, and pale in colour. This wasn't out of the ordinary for me. I'd grown up with this sort of oddity. I didn't much like it, but I got on with it.

As the four of us sat around the table that day, R's face was a picture. I loved R, but I also loved Mum. I watched R from the corner of my eye as I cut into the stringy flesh. She was silent, clearly working out what to do. To her credit, she attempted to eat it. But no muscle passed her lips. Eventually, she said, "I'm sorry, I can't eat it." I thought this might derail everything.

I can't remember what happened next, but it all turned out well. Mum's opinion of R was intact, even enhanced by her honesty. R also accepted Mum, although she was probably always doubtful about her culinary skills from thereon. I was relieved, and the visit was a success.

2 2

The call

I made enough progress on my engineering course at university to graduate. But along the way I had to retake a few exams. I never felt I had a handle on the core subjects of the course. I never mastered electrical engineering with its complicated maths and confusing practical work. I knew I'd never get a first-class honours degree; I just hoped I wouldn't be shamed and fail. All my assignments were handed in on time, even though I didn't understand what many of them meant. Along with others, I constructed projects on circuit boards that worked, but I was often never too sure why they worked. As I botched and bumbled my way along, I always felt somewhat behind the curve.

One of my proudest achievements was my ability to integrate mathematical equations using the Laplace transform (a method for solving complicated calculations). At the end of the year, I passed the exam without figuring out what Laplace transforms were all about. For my revision, I practised with examples from previous years' exam papers and learned to apply the method slavishly. Most of the time, it worked, even though I didn't have a clue what it all meant. I passed the exam, which was a great relief to me.

Many years later, when I was the rector of Macclesfield, a steady trickle of Indian Christians attended our Sunday services. They'd come to Britain to help with software development at the local pharmaceutical company. At the end of one service, I chatted with a couple. As I predicted, the husband was a software engineer on a six-month contract. His petite wife, who accompanied him, nestled their baby on her hip. Rather cheekily, I asked her what she got up to. Her reply astounded me as she told me she was a deputy professor in engineering maths on leave from her university in India. I'd made wrong assumptions about her. I asked if she understood Laplace transforms. Not only did she understand them, she taught them! I was immediately in awe of her; she was much more than a demure wife. So much for my so-called feminist credentials. She taught what I never got close to understanding, let alone mastering.

My struggle with Laplace and his mind-boggling transforms summed up much of my struggle with other parts of life. Many matters appeared beyond my grasp, not least my struggle with my faith. It meant so much to me, yet it was plain bonkers to many people I cared about and admired. I understood their confusion and inability to adopt what I held dear. In their shoes, I'd feel the same.

I fared no better on my industrial placements. I was unable to make sense of the electronics I was presented with. A small team might be asked to look at a circuit diagram of an instrument that wasn't working. Our job was to work out what was wrong and suggest a modification. My colleagues would examine the circuit diagram's lines, symbols and notes. Then, they'd make intelligent comments and propose various solutions to the problem. For me, the electronic drawing was usually about as clear as a foreign language I had not yet learned. I knew I was struggling to make progress.

While I calculated there was a chance I'd pass my final year exams, I never deluded myself into believing that I could become a competent engineer. I realized that working in electronics wasn't going to be for me.

In a semi-panic, I began to wonder and worry about my options. R and I were engaged to be married. My course ended in 12 months. What would I do?

Then, one Sunday evening, I was at a meeting, crammed into a house with many other young people, as we'd heard the speaker had a good story to tell. I can't remember what he said about his work in Kenya or the difference it made to the people in his neighbourhood. I can't remember what effect the work had on him. All I remember him saying was, "More people are needed in full-time Christian work." I've no idea whether he prefaced it with, "I think . . . " or "God says . . . " It wouldn't have made much difference if he had. The only way I can describe what happened was that I felt "fingered" (but not in the wrong way). I came away from there later that evening with a distinct impression I should do something about this. I wondered if I should get ordained in the church.

Many things happened. But in short, I spoke to my vicar, Max, who spoke to his bishop, who sent me away on a three-day selection conference in London. This was to work out if it was right to train me as a priest in the Church of England. After a programme of discussions, debates and interviews interspersed with a monastery-style pattern of services, the panel of selectors wrote a report to the bishop. The bishop passed it to my vicar. They concluded that they were uncertain about me. They weren't convinced I was ready to go forward for training.

The bishop and his officers prevaricated. The report sat in his in-tray for a long time. Then, my vicar, Max, lost his cool with the bishop over what he saw as an unnecessary delay. He pointed out I'd offered my life in service of the church; I was about to graduate and get married, yet no decision had been made. Max's passionate outburst removed the logjam. The bishop asked me to come in to see him. After a brief conversation, it was agreed I could go to theological college on the condition I first graduated in engineering.

At the age of 23, having not resolved the matter of my uneasiness with my faith, I was on the way to study theology in London. I asked myself if this was a good idea. Could this cure the embarrassment and awkwardness which had dogged me since I was 11?

So many times, I'd tried to do what I thought was right. I'd owned up about my faith to my university roommate. I'd taken a full part in the Christian mission on campus. And I faced the real possibility of becoming a vicar. It seemed like I was raising the stakes at each stage.

I wondered, if I couldn't solve this crisis, would my life eventually tumble out of control? Would this happen at the vicar college? Would it be humiliating? Or would I escape my embarrassment once and for all?

2 3

Our new start

University life ended and Toller, as we knew it and loved it, was wound up. An era was over and we were to go our separate ways.

On a warm summer afternoon, we all graduated. My degree pass wasn't spectacular, but I was relieved to get something. In the Great Hall, I crossed the platform and shook the Rt Hon Harold Wilson's hand. My family and friends clapped enthusiastically, and I left the hall a graduate, relieved.

A week later, we were married, celebrating with family and friends in the Liverpudlian sun. We got away from the reception that evening without our car getting the usual "Just Married" makeover, common in those days. But our smugness soon evaporated when its engine seized partway along the M56 motorway. It was, therefore, late into the night when we finally arrived at the cottage on a quiet stretch of the north Wales coast.

The first full day of our marriage was a Sunday. As any good Christian couple should, we went to the local church for the evening service. It was far from full, and, for some strange reason, we sat on the front row. Then, in full view of the minister and choir, we realized the service was to be in Welsh. R knew some rudimentary bits and pieces having been born over the border not far from Chester. I, however, was a foreigner. I didn't understand most of what happened that evening. Like my non-churchgoing friends back in the homeland, I felt the full force of what it was to be an alien on somebody else's religious territory.

Two weeks later, we set up home in London, off the Kilburn High Road. We'd started on something new. We'd moved south so I could train to become a vicar, a priest in the Church of England. I know, I know, it was a mad idea. Why would I, a timid Christian, put myself in such a position? This was either a mistake, foolishness or a bold move. Like my move up to grammar school, I was curious if another error might have been made in my favour. I understood the selection panel I'd faced was quite unsure about me. But still, I was recommended for training by the bishop.

I was surprised and somewhat alarmed to see where life landed me. The die was now cast; there was to be no going back.

ORDINAND

2 4

Doing God

I went to London to think about God; this is what theology is. For three years, along with 80 other students, I did my thinking in an idyllic setting surrounded by splendid grounds and a small wood. Not many have the chance to do this. Not many would choose to do this. I'm not sure how much choice I had in the matter.

Life took on a trajectory of its own. I felt like I was speeding down a ramp onto a ride that could both exhilarate and terrify me. I travelled with a sense of what I once heard referred to as reluctant nihilism: "If it is all going to go bad, well, let's get it over and done with." There was hope, but I didn't dare look too far into the future. I was happy because I was married; I felt sure we were in this together. Good companionship and a new start added a rich layer to our love.

Thinking about God for three years was to be something more than sitting around waiting for inspiration to turn up. Doing theology involved studying what many others say about God, Christianity and religion. It drew on the insights of the Bible's original authors, significant scholars, history, contemporary practice, science and the world at large. It had to do with how we understood and encountered God.

Intertwined with my reluctance was some anticipation; I hoped to resolve my internal conflict. I wanted this to end my embarrassment with faith. I longed for a resolution.

2 5

Theological college

The college was a world of its own. At the end of a driveway alongside a field of grazing cattle, it was far away from the main road's relentless drone of traffic and London's restless spirit. I'd arrived at one of the establishments where the future clergy of the Church of England were shaped and formed. I'd come to where I hoped men (yes, men in those days) became more certain and courageous about God and the stuff of faith.

As I started, I was both resistant and willing. On the one hand, something inside me wanted to do all I could not to be drawn too deeply into the world of the church. This would only distance me further from those I felt uncomfortable with yet nonetheless admired and loved. I also needed to take the chance to resolve my inner turmoil, which crippled me and left me being less than honest.

R and I lived two miles away from the campus. This suited me. It meant I could maintain some distance from what took place at college. It prevented me from becoming overwhelmed by its culture. I could've thrown in my lot with it all, become churchy and religious, burying my embarrassment for good. But I knew this wasn't for me. This wouldn't be an authentic way to live.

Some aspects of the college's routines were based upon the old traditions of Oxford and Cambridge. No gowns were worn, but there was a common room. Elements of Oxbridge traditions became evident at mealtimes. There was no cafeteria; there was a dining hall. Long tables, which seated 16, were set out along it. At the head of the room was a longer table on a raised platform. The principal sat at its centre, overlooking everything and everyone. No one sat to eat their meal until he took his seat. He didn't take his seat until he'd rung a small bell and a prayer of thanksgiving for the food had been said.

In one way, I accepted this stuffiness. It was the way things were done. I assumed I'd have to learn these quirky ways. After all, many clergy successfully trained here, so who was I to throw it all over? At another level, I felt a resistance growing within me. This wasn't a world I was used to or wished to get used to. There might have been a common room, but the setup wasn't common enough for me.

Emblazoned on the wall behind the principal's seat in the dining hall was a coat of arms. At the base of it was the college's motto: "Be right and persist." Like the words of the plaques I found uncomfortable in my family home, this strapline bore down on me several times a day for three years. It wasn't an easy message to forget.

I was a 23-year-old with little life experience or wisdom. I didn't realize I'd moved into a world that attempted to reinforce my inherited beliefs and values rather than help me examine and critique them. An assumption among most of the staff was that there was a set of non-negotiables to "Be right" about. It was a version of Christianity which saw itself as superior to other forms and, therefore, critical of them.

Even then, this intense desire to be right didn't rest easily with me. I couldn't help but think it was rooted in insecurity rather than strength. It was as if I was being nurtured, even groomed, into a way of being compassionate towards our own but antagonistic towards those we disagreed with. One student, an Anglo-Catholic, felt like a fish out of water. But to his credit, he stuck at it. All who held more liberal theological views were also regarded with some suspicion.

I'd entered a world I struggled to make sense of. Some aspects of college made me feel uneasy. At times, I didn't know what to think. This only added to my sense of unease and disquiet. The plot got thicker.

2 6

Plagiarism and the poor

Apart from a couple of years in my late teens, I struggled with education. Behind me was a stream of poor results and some failures.

I knew I wasn't stupid, but that was the feeling I got when teachers and lecturers commented on my work. Now in London, I'd moved on to yet more education when most of my friends had already shouted "good riddance!" as they left university.

I relate to the adage: "I love learning, but I hate being taught."

Having somehow made the grade, foxed the selectors or duped the bishop, I was committed to a further three years of study on another degree course. My first degree mainly involved maths. When my son took maths in the sixth form, his whimsical teacher would sigh, "Ah, maths, the lazy man's language." Not much needed to be written. In four years of studying engineering, I wrote one essay of only 1,200 words. Now, I was on an essay-based course.

To an outsider, it must have looked as if I was deliberately trying to make things difficult for myself. Not only was I aggravating the situation with my unease about being a Christian, but I was also setting out on a course I wasn't well-suited for. I feared I wouldn't cope.

My first assignment was a 2,500-word essay. This was an enormous number of words for me. The task was to critique some aspects of Marx and Engels' *Communist Manifesto*. I was prepared to be as left-wing as any other student, but this manifesto wasn't a passionate call to action but a dreary analysis of the class struggle. After much procrastination and the pushing around of words on the page, I typed up my submission and handed it in. A week later, the tutor passed me in the corridor. "Oh, Graham, about your essay, I have it here. It isn't good enough; you'll have to rewrite it." He handed me my work and walked on. On the last page was the mark: 28 per cent.

Students nowadays are more savvy. They'd hunt down the tutor, ask them to justify why they'd awarded such a low mark before finding out how to improve the piece. It didn't even cross my mind to do either. I accepted it in the spirit it was given to me and walked on to where I was heading. I'd been well nurtured in deferential behaviour.

Growing up, I was taught to be submissive and polite to my elders. I'd believed those "over me" would tell people like me what I needed to know when I required it. "They", after all, were the ones who knew. This acquiescence tainted all aspects of my life, not least my understanding about faith, God, the Bible, the church and everything else I was immersed in. All I needed to do (as a humble Christian) was to learn how to receive from those who knew better than me. If there were any problems, they'd most likely be my fault. This only served to accommodate my embarrassment about faith in my life.

For future assignments, I knew I needed a strategy if I was going to survive the course. Copying out of the set textbooks clearly wasn't allowed. Rephrasing what the books said would also be rumbled.

Then, I discovered the basement of the library. Going down the metal spiral staircase led to shelves full of obscure books no one used. Most of them were out-of-date, donated by vicars' widows as they cleared out their husbands' studies. These were my only hope. It was worth the risk. I didn't know what else I could do. I decided to write my essays by copying sections from these books (or rewriting them as best I could in my own words). I was confident that, even if the tutors had read them, they wouldn't remember what was in them.

I soon received my next assignment. It was about the structure of the Old Testament. Back in my study, I scanned the recommended textbooks. They were too big to read, and I was a slow reader. So, I went to the library and down the spiral steps to the shelves of the more obscure books. Finding some I guessed might do, I stitched together parts of chapters I thought addressed the set question. I wasn't too sure if this would work. I reached the required number of words, typed up my scribblings, popped the result into the tutor's pigeonhole, and hoped for the best.

Two weeks later, I received a mark of 47 per cent. My strategy worked. I was more than relieved. No one realized what I was up to. My marks were poor, but at least they were passes. I got by, which is what mattered to me. It was years later I discovered this was called plagiarism.

*

The assumption behind much of the training wasn't a lot different to Billy Graham's question, "If you were to die tonight, do you know where you are going?" As would-be vicars, we were being trained to entice non-Christians to become "born-again" believers so they could answer the evangelist's question and fill up our churches. Even though we had, in theory, studied Marx and Engels, the social context in which we were being asked to work, once ordained, didn't impact how we were taught. The view was everyone needed to become Christians, just as we were. This was the bottom line.

This approach was true for most of the tutors, although one made my ears prick up and take notice. On several occasions in his class, the New Testament tutor, talking about the Gospel of Luke, mentioned that this Gospel demonstrated a bias towards the poor. He said Luke embraced a concern for all who suffered economically, people in debt and those oppressed by others. This was music to my ears. Never before had I heard anything like this. It was radical talk in those days. This wasn't about a Jesus whose sole interest was getting folk into a religious experience with God so they'd go to heaven when they died. This was about a Jesus who addressed the concerns of the many who suffered in the here and now.

I'd been fed a line that suggested people had only themselves to blame for refusing to become Christians; they chose not to believe. In some quarters, this was extended to the view that poor people were responsible for the poverty they suffered. Abundance and success were then signs of God's blessing. I grew up in a church environment where the rich were admired rather than questioned. Being a Westerner, I was, of course, rich.

I could see why many non-church people I knew wouldn't sign up to this brand of religion. They weren't to be blamed; I started to wonder if they should be congratulated.

One person who refused to believe was Sue, a colleague of R's. They were fellow pharmacists at the local hospital. Sue was a New Zealander, an atheist and a feminist. As part of my ethics module, I was required to give a presentation to the rest of the class on a topical issue. As Chas' mum had had such an impact on my thinking, I chose feminism.

When R chatted about this engaging person, Sue, I was intrigued. I suggested we invite her around so I could pick her brains for my presentation. She came, and we plied her with food and wine.

Sue was thoughtful, passionate about the plight of women and willing to help me, a vicar in training, with my seminar. She was another of those outsiders I had great respect for. But, of course, she didn't "do God". R and I couldn't deny there was something good about her—was not this goodness God?

My fellow students thought presenting the case for feminism in a patriarchal institution was either brave or foolish. It was probably both. Several students' wives came in to listen to my presentation. In those days, I was far from confident about speaking in public. I prepared as best I could and told myself to slow down, to speak unhurriedly and carefully. Even so, my residual stammer tripped me up a little.

After my 15-minute input, there were a few questions. Some could've been construed as hostile if I'd been feeling sensitive. But I was okay. I thought it went well.

On our way down to the dining hall for lunch, following the class, the tutor made a beeline for me. I braced myself, but he was graciousness itself. He thanked me for what I'd said; he thought I'd made a compelling case.

What I hadn't expected was the adverse reaction from some of the wives who attended. They felt I had undermined the God-given pattern of how relationships should be ordered. Women weren't equal to men and shouldn't be ordained in the church, was their view.

Strangely, I was happy there was some opposition. If I'm honest, something in me likes to go against the grain. At least it meant I hadn't been banal or bland—two things I'm intolerant of in others.

I was also happy for another reason. It confirmed that I wasn't unwilling to stand up for what I believed to be right, even in the face of resistance or opposition. I realized I didn't mind being marginalized as long as I knew there was a good reason for it. Whenever I'd been asked to stand up and defend my faith, as it was usually presented, there seemed to be no good reason to do it. I liked a fight, but it had to be a decent fight.

As my course progressed, I realized the "system", the college's way of doing things (and many established and popular Christian ways), wouldn't work for me. It dawned on me I'd have to find my own path through life and discover my way of inhabiting the faith. But I was clueless as to what I should do about it. I didn't realize that this was to be a long journey, one on which I'd end up ditching the label "Christian" while still attempting to follow the maverick, Jesus.

Even though I was embarrassed about aspects of my faith and the culture of the church, I couldn't leave this Jesus to one side. There was something so compelling about him. If I dropped him, what could I put in place that would be his equal?

2 7

Chapel

If I was to be a vicar, it was fair enough to expect that I would be able to pray; it was, after all, part of the job. However, I'd never been much good at praying; it was a weakness I decided I needed to put right.

The college day ran between two chapel services, one at 7:20 am and the other at 5:30 pm. This wasn't handy for those of us living off campus. When we first moved to London, our flat was a 40-minute drive away. To get to the morning service on time, we had to leave by 6:30 am. Squeezing into our two-cylinder Fiat 126, we trundled across the relatively deserted streets of north London. R then sat in my study, trying to come around from the shock of such an early start before going on to work a few miles away while I sat in the chapel, trying to come around from the shock of such a rude awakening. The words and music wafted around me in my sleepy daze. If I was meeting God at these morning appointments, the encounters left a lot to be desired.

I tried, I really tried. I gave this morning praying routine my best shot. But it is hard to do anything when you are tired. It is hard to be nice to fellow students, staff or God when you're so played out, when all you want to do is sleep.

I tried with the evening services too, but alas, again without success. As the evenings drew in with the progress of winter, darkness crept into the chapel and into my spirit. We weren't getting home until after 7:00 pm. These days were over 12 hours long.

Being open and loving to others is hard when you feel resentful. I resented the fact that most students and all the staff lived on campus. They could roll out of bed shortly before the morning service started and go home afterwards to doze on the sofa with a cup of tea until lectures started at 9:00 am. (As there was limited student accommodation, those of us married without children had to live off campus.)

I resented the fact that I was expected to attend chapel twice a day and hang around until the evening service finished at 6:00 pm. My hope to become a better pray-er was regressing rather than developing. I was in no frame of mind to pray. I was also in no frame of mind to study.

Looking back, I'm amazed I never complained to the staff about this. They seemed remote, even overly serious, most of the time. Maybe it was because I was only 23 years old and still immature but, once again, I deferred to them. I couldn't seem to connect with them.

As I didn't question anything openly, I decided all I could do was to keep my head down and survive. I, therefore, attended morning chapel three times a week and the evening service twice. Others, I noticed, started to follow a similar pattern.

At the beginning of each term, the principal gave us a pep talk in which he strongly encouraged us to attend chapel, otherwise, he said, we'd never survive the rigours of parish life. Well, I wasn't surviving the rigours of college life.

Although nothing was said to me personally, I felt the criticism. It embedded within me a sense of guilt. Guilt doesn't help any sort of relationship develop, especially a relationship with God reliant on prayer. Many years later, I heard the freedom-giving words, "Pray as you can, not as you can't." These were from a monk who knew all about the downsides of the intense prayer routines of a monastery. For my part, I decided I had to attempt to leave my guilt behind.

The sternness of the services and the motto on the coat of arms in the dining hall made me wonder what I was becoming a part of. My resistance grew as my willingness flagged.

2 8

Keeping rooted

Halfway through my time, I knew I needed to do something outside of college and church to keep me from being consumed by their worlds. I was in danger of becoming overwhelmed. I longed to do something, anything, "ordinary". R agreed. We got a brochure from the local authority listing all the evening classes in our neighbourhood from which she opted for upholstery and I chose car maintenance. We paid our money and enrolled.

Every Thursday evening, we'd set off on the five-mile journey to another college. It felt as if we were back in the real world. Sitting alongside me as I learnt how to service an engine and grind in new valves were the folk I was at ease with. On warm evenings, we checked out each other's cars and told tales of the different jobs we'd attempted. I liked mechanical things, I understood them. Also, I found it easy to chat with other blokes about cars.

I wanted a faith that could be expressed and understood in a similarly straightforward manner. It needed to make sense, even when chatting across the open bonnet of a car. But the Christianity I knew was too otherworldly. It used words, images and ideas most people didn't use: heaven, grace, redemption, worship, angels, blessing, salvation, faith, etc. It was complex to explain, and if I tried, it was hard not to sound like a religious nut.

At one level, it was odd that I signed up for the evening class because others there were bound to ask what I did. I could say I was a student. Then, they'd ask what my subject was. And before you knew it, I'd have to admit I was a vicar in the making. Then, the whole embarrassment thing would kick off again.

I didn't only attend the evening class because I needed a break from my theological training. It was also as if I had to put myself in a position where I'd feel uncomfortable and out of sorts. I suppose one reason was to make sure that I still felt uncomfortable identifying as a Christian. The other part was to check I hadn't surrendered myself so much to a religious system that I no longer cared. I wanted to care; I wanted, in some way, to feel a degree of disquiet. This was crucial for my integrity. I wanted to show up as the real me, as best I could, with my outer life reflecting my inner life.

*

Friday night chapel was a big deal. It was the evening of the preaching service which we were all expected to attend; wives often came too if they were able. Each week, a well-known name was invited to speak. Out of all the men (yes, yes, it was only men) who spoke, only one has stuck in my memory. His name was Michael Marshall, the then Bishop of Woolwich. It was a courageous move for the college as he was from the Anglo-Catholic wing of the church, a section of the church who believed other stuff to us evangelicals. For me, from what happened during that evening, it was clear those differences didn't matter.

This man spoke with a clarity and conviction I'd never heard before. He wasn't patronizing, or parsonic. Instead, the overall impression I got was that he was genuine and well-rooted, comfortable in his own skin. There was something straightforward about him and, in his honesty, he spoke about what he didn't know as well as what he knew. I sensed a ring of authenticity that I had not seen in anyone else.

What struck so many of us present that night wasn't any great thought, teaching or insight but his passion, energy and love. I'm not given much to tears, but he made me cry that evening. I wanted what he had.

As he spoke, it became clear that what I coveted in him had been hard-won. This wasn't the fruit of ever-growing achievement and success. It had come through his pain, his failures and the hard knocks he'd suffered. I couldn't help but warm to him. His vulnerability drew me and others to him.

When R and I came away from the service, I felt comforted and disturbed. It strangely left me with a deeper commitment to my forthcoming ordination, and any disruption I felt seemed to be an essential part of the process. I was surer than ever that I *must* become a vicar. I wondered (and feared) whether my path through life might also include suffering and failure at some stage. Maybe my life would fall apart one day, only then to be remade.

No matter what happened, I wanted to live a well-rooted life. What would life have in store for me, I wondered.

CURATE

2 9

Holy orders

As the end of college approached, there was a feverish mood among us would-be vicars. We were eager to get fixed up with our first job, known as a curacy. This on-the-job training post typically lasted five or six years. I was to become a curate.

I was thrilled when my friend Steve Allen, a vicar in Leeds, persuaded his bishop to let me join him there. I was relieved I'd secured a post.

Sensing potential sales, clergy outfitters with eccentric-sounding names like Wippels, Vanpoulles and Hayes & Finch began to appear at college. Students buzzed around the room where they held their sales like bees around a honey pot to see what caught their eye. They tried on clerical shirts, surplices, cassocks, scarves, stoles and other miscellaneous bits and pieces, all deemed necessary for parish life.

A few of us never attended these fayres. I'm unsure why others didn't; I knew why I avoided them. They provoked a mixed sense of terror, embarrassment and (almost) revulsion in me. I couldn't get excited about the whole clergy role/look package.

My colleagues admired each other as they posed vicar-like. I was pleased that they were pleased, but I couldn't get involved myself. Even though the staff insisted these bits and bobs were necessary to be a minister in the church, I was more than doubtful about what I thought to be these non-essentials. I couldn't shake from my mind the boys at school, the men on the factory shop floor, those I sat with at my evening class, and many more I knew and loved. I couldn't get away from what they'd think of me, and how wary most of them would be about the clergy role/look package.

Eventually, before we set off for Yorkshire, I ordered two clergy shirts by post. These were the only proper clerical items I ever bought. My other shirts were supplied by Marks & Spencer and adapted by R. They never looked quite right; it didn't bother me.

After the visits of the flamboyant clergy outfitters, the next excitement at college was over ordination cards. This was a well-established tradition.

Students had printed small, immaculately produced cards that informed their family, friends and acquaintances they'd soon be ordained. They gave details about the ceremony, when and where it would take place, in case anyone wanted to attend. At the bottom were the words "Please pray for me". I had a problem with this.

This was my problem: I didn't regard my calling as any more worthy than anyone else's. I didn't think getting ordained was on a higher plane than any other vocation. It wasn't nobler; all callings in life are noble. I was sure my fellow students hadn't ordered similar cards when previously they'd been on the verge of becoming nurses, shopkeepers or astrophysicists. I doubted any of them asked their family and friends to pray for them like this. In my mind, the business over ordination cards bolstered the notion that we, as potential clergy, were somehow moving onto a higher, more spiritual level. It reinforced in me the idea that we were becoming more unintelligible to those we wanted to connect with, who themselves were increasingly incredulous about us.

I was glad to leave college and pleased we were going to Leeds, but I feared what lay ahead.

I never returned for the graduation service as I'd had enough of religious fuss, especially of the evangelical kind. The college posted my degree certificate rolled up in a cardboard tube. Enclosed with it was a testimonial from the principal, which I was to show to my bishop before he could ordain me. It confirmed I'd completed my training and said I was ready for the "Holy Office of Deacon". The testimonial read: "He hath in every way proved himself exemplary in conduct and deportment." Deportment, as I understood it, was about how a person stood and walked; it had something to do with etiquette. This was bizarre. It continued: "He hath never, so far as we know, said, or written anything contrary to the Doctrine or Discipline of the Church of England." Somehow, I'd made the grade. It was all systems go. I was ready to be ordained.

The ordination service was a grand affair held at the imposing cathedral in Ripon, where I and 12 other men would be transformed into clergymen. Getting ready for the day was much like getting ready for a wedding. There was a lot of preparation to do, legal papers to sign off, and a lengthy rehearsal to attend.

The central part of the preparation was a retreat: three nights away with my fellow ordinands. Staying at the Archbishop of York's palace, I was immersed in another world. It was a magnificent, listed building surrounded by well-maintained grounds alongside the River Ouse. It exuded an old-fashioned opulence. While I was there, I wasn't too sure how to behave. I didn't know what to say to the archbishop at mealtimes. "Out of my depth" didn't start to describe how I felt. If my non-church friends had seen me, it would've confirmed their worst fears about Christianity and the church. It confirmed many of mine.

We spent time in quiet reflection each day, attending services and walking the grounds, although it rained a lot. On the evening before the ordination service, we were called to the chapel for the Archbishop's Charge. Although it sounded like a lively jousting event, it was far from that. It was a formal message from the archbishop. We were instructed to come dressed in our cassocks, the long black gowns clergy often wear during services.

In our awkwardness, we sat in silence until he arrived. Then, as instructed, we stood. It was then I realized something was wrong. As I scanned my fellow ordinands there that evening, it was clear that the double breast on my cassock closed the opposite way to everyone else's. Their cassocks were all closed left over right; mine was right over left. Some, I noticed, spotted that mine was different.

To save money, I hadn't bought a proper cassock from one of the suppliers. But as I needed one, R said she could make one for me by adapting a choir girl's cassock pattern. She deftly sewed together what I needed and assured me no one would notice—but they did.

It felt like a sign of things to come. Little did I guess how much I'd be travelling against the grain of the church's culture in the years that followed. R offered to put the cassock right, but I preferred its quirkiness.

The next day, I travelled with Tim from the palace to the cathedral. Conspicuous didn't start to describe how I felt as I wore my clerical collar (often called a dog collar). I wondered where all this would end.

In the chapter house of the cathedral, I swore an oath to be faithful and bear true allegiance to the Queen before the service got underway. It was a bit hard to swallow for someone with republican leanings. I didn't recall anyone telling me I'd need to do this. Years later, I heard Tony Benn

MP say that this was the "forced lie" he was required to make to take up his seat in the House of Commons. I also swore to obey the bishop in all things lawful and honest. That was a bit easier to live with.

Then, processing out into the grand nave of the cathedral, the service got underway. Family and friends looked on. As part of the long, convoluted service, I knelt before the bishop as he prayed for me. Finally, I came out into the sunshine as a Clerk in Holy Orders, my new legal status.

I was now a clergyman.

3 0

Alice in Wonderland

When I started working with Steve Allen in Leeds, I felt I'd landed on my feet. I knew we'd get on well. While this was all very exciting, it also added an extra layer of discomfort to my awkwardness. If I was to make any sense to atheists, agnostics and sceptics, there was now even more to overcome. While I felt embarrassed about my faith in their company, I still didn't understand the depth of their incredulity towards people like me.

In my early years, growing up in a Christian household, I was blind to how outsiders viewed us as insiders. I'd unquestioningly accepted many ideas and beliefs. I had to; that's how growing up works. I moved in and out and between different ideas and images, many of which, on the face of it, didn't make much sense together. Indeed, some seemed contradictory.

The Bible's assumption that the universe consisted of three levels didn't bother me. I was used to talking about heaven being "up there" and the place where the dead go as "down there". These themes were familiar to me since we recited them in the creeds and liturgies every week at church.

It didn't bother me when we read about some people living almost a thousand years or the two men who never died, as they were "taken up". We listened to stories about angels, sea monsters, columns of smoke and pillars of fire as if these were everyday events.

It also didn't bother me when Jesus' disciples found the money they needed to pay their tax bill in a fish's mouth or that a virgin could become pregnant. I'd grown up in a faith rooted in this.

However, if anyone published an article in a magazine claiming the earth was flat, sea monsters threatened our shipping and money grew on trees (or in fish), I'd say they were crazy.

I hadn't appreciated how deft I'd become at navigating between the Bible's worldview and my scientific-based understanding of the world. But the disparity between the ancient and the contemporary worlds wasn't yet too much of a problem for me; I could still function.

I say all this wasn't too much of a problem for me until a non-religious acquaintance criticized me for holding such views. But even then, I wasn't aware of the depth of scepticism these friends had towards my beliefs. I continued to operate as an insider. I hadn't realized the depth of the intellectual problem I, or the church, was facing.

But still, I couldn't throw off the feeling that my friends were shaking their heads in disbelief behind my back, saying, "He seems like a nice guy, how come he believes this nonsense?"

I lived with a terrible tension. My faith meant so much to me, but I was aware others viewed it as a fantasy world, much like *Alice in Wonderland*.

As the way we talked about God meant more to insiders than outsiders, I spent more time with insiders. This was cowardice; I thought my embarrassment with my faith was primarily my fault, my lack of courage.

I was yet to realize that people hadn't necessarily gone off God; they'd gone off the language we used to talk about God and faith in an age aware of science.

So, I continued with my split, schizophrenic mindset while longing for a resolution to my distress. I never spoke about it as it felt like shame.

3 1

Church buildings

While the chapel dominated my college life, once ordained, church buildings dominated my working life. These were a heavy presence, a burden to carry. They exaggerated all my embarrassments about faith and gave home to my awkwardness. Their images and subliminal messages didn't make much sense to me, let alone to my "outside" friends. They overpowered the church's culture to such an extent they muted what I saw as Jesus' radical agenda of social reform, human flourishing and personal freedom.

Many of my clergy colleagues argue that plenty of non-church people like church buildings and find them helpful. While *some* people, like the comedian and humanist Sandi Toksvig, enjoy the peaceful atmosphere of a church, I've found that many of my atheist, agnostic and sceptical friends view our buildings in a more negative light. On balance, these structures work against the teachings of Jesus rather than for them. As I understand the Gospels, Jesus didn't seem impressed with any buildings. When his men pointed out how mighty their great cathedral was (sorry, Temple), he told them to drop their wonder because the whole thing would come crashing down in the not-too-distant future. He never arranged tours of synagogues, as we might do with church buildings today. He said, if there was going to be worship in the future, it wouldn't be on anyone's hill or in anyone's building. Instead, it would come from the heart of the community, people's relationships.

Throughout my career, I've never harboured a fondness for any of the church buildings I've worked in. They've been a money sink. Their maintenance took up much of the clergy's attention and a lot of church members' time. Their inflexibility speaks of an understanding of faith which is not mine. Whenever there was a proposal to reorder or rearrange a building, I was always a keen enthusiast.

For my curacy, R and I moved into a bungalow on a Leeds council estate. It was attached to a small multipurpose church building constructed 25 years earlier. It lacked many of the trappings you'd expect to discover in a church. There was a beaten-up simplicity about it; it had a certain attraction. However, even here, the small congregation nurtured an aspiration to make it look like a "proper church" inside. So, on Saturdays, pews were pulled into position alongside a small lectern and a simple altar to prepare it for the Sunday service. A small harmonium organ was also dragged into position since the regulars believed there should be an organ, despite the presence of a piano.

I don't know how much you know about harmoniums, but they are foot-powered squeeze boxes with a keyboard standing less than half the height of a piano. They sound like small organs. Over time, though, they tend to go out of tune. As most are decades old, they are usually wildly out of kilter. This device would wheeze and puff during each service as it accompanied the small congregation's singing. It was an assault on the hearing of anyone who had any appreciation of music and an embarrassment if anyone came in off the street to visit.

A few of us became obsessed with this instrument and wanted to get rid of it. But it was up to the local church committee to decide, not us—and they loved it. One evening, after a few beers, Nick (a mature university student with whom I ran the youth group) and I hatched a plan. If the harmonium couldn't be got rid of by legal means, how about illicit means? So, once we had plucked up courage, and armed with a screwdriver and a Stanley knife, we passed through the adjoining door from our house into the church building. Everything was set up for the next day. We went straight to the harmonium and unscrewed its back panel, exposing two leather bellows. In a manic and inebriated state, Nick took the knife and slashed at the leather lungs. Laughing uncontrollably and astounded at our audacity, we reinstated the rear panel, pushed the instrument back into its position, and retreated through the adjoining door, closing it behind us. Steve, as vicar, was due to take the service the following day.

He and I met every Monday to sort out the work for the coming week and review how the weekend went. As we chatted, he said, "A funny thing happened yesterday down at the Heights Estate church. Tony sat to play the first hymn, but nothing came out of the harmonium." Steve seemed puzzled yet pleased; he also despised the instrument. I couldn't help myself. I burst out laughing and confessed. Steve was okay with that.

It all backfired, however. The following week, Tony turned up with his toolkit to see why it wasn't working. On opening up the machine, he was dismayed. "Who has done this?" We stroked our chins and faked concern, saying we had no idea how such a thing could have happened. The last laugh was on us. Tony loved this harmonium and spent hours repairing it and putting it right. From then on, it was louder and more out of tune than ever!

Why can't we see how the lunacy of our religious practices appears to those on the outside? Regular church members ask why new people do not come to church, as if nothing absurd happens in them.

If I do have a favourite church building, it is the Gallarus Oratory out on the Dingle Peninsula in the west of Ireland. Built in 1756, it is no more than a shelter of rounded stones. There's no mortar between them. There's nowhere to sit, no door and no flooring, except for the trodden earth. At the east end is a simple window with no frame or glazing. The altar is a large chunk of rock in front of it. With a squeeze, there is just enough room for ten people to stand, huddled together. No razzmatazz, no flash imagery, no ego statements, plenty of simplicity and strength, and a sense of wonder. To me, it embodies the spirit of Jesus.

Growing up within the church, I heard the point made time and time again, "The church is not the building, but the people." Yet, we persist in calling these ecclesiastical structures "churches".

Early in my first parish, I vowed never to call them "churches", if at all possible.

Over the years, I've felt imprisoned by these buildings, yet unable to work without them. I also felt misunderstood because of them. On their school visits, teachers emphasized to the children everything I thought was superfluous and passed over what I thought most important: the death and resurrection nature of life. When God was mentioned, it was implied that God was more present in these human structures than anywhere else. I never believed that.

Years later, when I asked a bishop if we could rename a building "The Main Building" instead of "Church" during a redesign and refurbishment project, the core sentence of his reply read, "While I admire your iconoclastic zeal, the answer is no."

As I'm not much into church buildings, I don't seek them out when I'm on holiday. If I do enter one, it is usually to find some peace. However, their powerful, unspoken voices often break into my silence and unsettle me once again.

Their music also adds to my awkwardness. I once heard someone say at a party, "If you want to be a churchgoer, you need to be into a medieval or a *kum bay ya* style of music." While many insiders find these forms helpful, I knew they weren't the genres of choice for most people. Some churches try to get around this by putting on a rock concert-styled service for their main Sunday event. One friend (an ex-born-again Christian) said to me, "If I want to go to a rave, I'll go to a rave, not a church service. If I go to church, I want to encounter mystery." I understand where she's coming from. She's no longer a Christian but a pagan minister.

Church buildings serve many purposes, but they cannot love. Only people can love. Love is what we are ultimately drawn to.

The power of church buildings has been hard to ignore. While I've experienced plenty of great times in them, their weight of presence has distracted me from moments of wonder and awe.

3 2

Success and discomfort

Once settled into parish life, I was surprised how well I functioned. I expected to fail and collapse into an incoherent heap. I know self-praise is often a sign of insecurity, but with support from my vicar-friend Steve and his wife, Liz, I thrived. So much happened: small study groups developed and grew, the youth group started to fill the cellar where we met, folk seemed to like me, the church building was reordered, the music moved forward, more worshippers began to attend and ITV came to televise our morning service. Although I didn't do it all, I played a significant role. I never expected to get on so well. Even my jumbled-up public speaking style improved.

However, not only did I operate within my two worldviews effortlessly, but I did it unconsciously. And unconsciously, I expected those who decided to become Christians would be able to navigate both of these worlds as I did. While some learned to ride this two-horse race, many didn't. We hadn't provided them with a way of making sense of an ancient worldview of life while living in a scientific and postmodern context. This made it easy for critics to dismiss Christianity as only for the lost or those who needed a crutch. So this was one of those times when I felt we were often pitied.

In hindsight, I can see how ill-equipped I was to deal with this. Nothing I studied at theological college prepared me. My training emphasized helping outsiders understand the church and its message. Maybe it should've been more about the church understanding and reading the world. For hundreds of years, Christians have said there are two books we must read: the Bible and the World. While I wasn't good at understanding the Bible, I was even worse at making sense of the world.

As a curate, I thought my main business was growing the church. Everyone likes to belong to something that looks as if it's thriving. I was young and enthusiastic.

*

Over the centuries, Christians have fallen into the trap of dividing reality into two spheres: the spiritual and the natural. We've then made it our business to help people become more spiritual. This supported a view that believes everything natural is permanently tainted and most likely irredeemable. Alongside this was the idea we need to become less human. We even apologize, saying, "Sorry, I'm only human," as if our humanity is something to be apologetic for. We've turned being human into a weak, shameful thing. But to be truly human is to be as God made us to be.

With this misunderstanding, it is easy to preach Billy Graham's message about going to heaven when you die, as we can then leave this (terrible) world behind. As Christians, we've binged on separating the spiritual and the natural. I was guilty of jumping onto this bandwagon. But looking back, it was a mistake; it was dualistic thinking.

I shudder to think how I must have come across. I'm sure the way I communicated the message of Jesus was unintelligible to many I met in and around Leeds. Looking back, I regret how I presented myself as it only reinforced my discomfort with how others regarded me.

Though I found success as a curate, it didn't make it easier for me to wear the clerical collar or be a clergyman. Other clergy appeared to be at ease in their attire and the role. Each month, clergy across our side of the city met for support, to share news and find out what was happening in the wider church. These gatherings were called chapters. They might sound like Hell's Angels meetings, but no tattoos, bikes or leathers were ever on show.

I remember turning up for my very first meeting, arriving deliberately late as I didn't want to go. I didn't want to be counted as one among a band of clergy. I didn't want to be a cleric. I just wanted to do what I thought I must do—follow my calling. But to do this meant becoming one of what I considered this weird and uncomfortable breed of the ordained. My animosity towards the clerical image had been well nurtured as I grew up alongside my school friends and in the places where I'd worked.

Where we lived added to my sense of unease. Our quirky bungalow home, attached (in a semi-detached sort of way) to the beaten-up small church building, made us seem peculiar. Being on a hillside, it sat above the road and was looked down upon by the houses behind. Whether it was true or not, there was a feeling of being watched from all sides. Not being council-built, there was no other property like it on the estate.

So our house was different. I, being a clergyman, was different. As outsiders, R and I were different to the people of the estate. Apart from the handful who turned up each Sunday morning at nine o'clock, those who lived locally were not much interested in anything Christian or religious. It was a strange dynamic of awkwardness to live in, but I pressed on.

The strange bungalow became our home. It was where we began our family when Adrian and Becca came into our lives, making our lives so much the richer. This was the home where local kids ran across our flat roof as I changed nappies, making us feel vulnerable. But it was also the place of laughter and fun, where we shared food with friends and hosted a music group.

Then, I made some missteps.

33

Missteps

I basked in my success. I continued to emphasize the spiritual while becoming more aware of the credibility gap between my faith (with all its associated religious and ecclesiastical baggage) and where many, if not most, lived.

Let me tell you about my missteps.

My first was to assume that success was everything. Success is like a drug; once you've tasted it, especially after having experienced so little, you only want more. But this led me to assume I knew more than I did. Success felt like a shortcut to wisdom. Many applaud you and love you when you achieve and excel. There is, though, a reason why older, calmer and more wounded souls are able to speak a truth we don't want to hear when we're young. The truth is success has little true value to teach us. Undoubtedly, I needed some victories and accolades to help me get started and keep me from becoming discouraged. However, I didn't realize it, but taking my few achievements too seriously led me down a wild, unpredictable road.

Along with this first error was a wrong assumption I'd been taught during my Christian upbringing. This notion suggests that we need to be transformed into somebody different from who we already are. While many of us rightly want to change for the better, I was yet to discover that we didn't need to change into *different* people. We needed to become the people we *already* were but didn't yet know it. The centuries-old Christian belief calls this "the image of God" or, as I like to call it, "a chip off the old block".

I looked all around to find the person I thought I should be. I tried to emulate those who seemed to have achieved greater success and had fewer flaws than me. In truth, I had no idea who I was. In my excitement and enthusiasm, I led others down the same path.

My third mistake was to jump on the bandwagon that categorizes reality into two spheres. But like many others at the time, I took it on a stage further. Not only did I divide reality into the natural and the spiritual, but into the physical and the supernatural. I erroneously equated the spiritual with the supernatural. I wish I'd known what I know now: everything belongs in one reality. No one place is more God-filled than anywhere else.

My belief in a supernatural realm sent me down a wrong path. This approach meant nothing to my non-religious acquaintances. To them, it was just another reason to think I was beyond redemption. Despite this, the idea of witnessing supposedly supernatural events was too tempting for me (and many other Christians) to ignore. I found myself acting against my better judgement.

Around this time, another preacher arrived from southern California whose exciting Christian approach to healing appealed to many of us in the staid English church. John Wimber's "Signs and Wonders" conference ticked our supernatural box. It appealed to excitable Christianity, and it appealed to my ego.

Wimber was different from many who'd come across from the States peddling their versions of being miracle-workers. Unlike them, he seemed to be a nice guy, in a big daddy sort of way. From what I could tell, he was humble, often making self-deprecating remarks—a trait I've always warmed to in people. It suggested he was safe to be with.

He said he didn't want to be a miracle-worker. His goal was to help bring healing to the sick and suffering, emphasizing that anyone could get involved.

He was honest about what he didn't understand, his mistakes and that he needed a good team of people around him. He wasn't a one-man show. Honesty and humility are close bedfellows.

Wimber also changed the way I looked at the Bible. He helped me refocus on the Gospel accounts, which had been overshadowed by the emphasis on St Paul's writings, which I had been taught throughout my life.

As I started to reacquaint myself with the Gospel writings, I discovered a Jesus who was presented as wonderful, troublesome and controversial. At times, it felt as if I was reading these texts for the first time, even though I knew the stories well.

The challenging, confusing and life-affirming stories of Jesus helped move me on from my much-loved arguments for why I was right, arguments often based erroneously on the writings of St Paul. I was starting to find again that "something" which is more sensed than thought. I'd been here before.

We ended our time in Leeds on a wave of accomplishment. I was enthusiastic about moving on to have my own parish. We never expected to move south. But we did, to the unknown territory of inner-city Birmingham, where I'd become vicar. The Brummie accent was about to invade our lives. My embarrassment and awkwardness about who I was and what I believed travelled with me.

3 4

Job search

Securing a vicar's job in the Church of England is much like trying for any other job, whether as a postman, care worker or brain surgeon. Despite the claim to have God on our side, finding the right person for a post seems to be as much a gamble in the church as in any other sector.

The powers that be suggested I look at a couple of jobs in the middle of council estates in the north. We went to look at them, but R was hesitant, and she was right. We had already spent five years isolated on such an estate and we weren't ready to repeat it, with two infants, anytime soon. Another possibility came up in Liverpool, which I might have been interested in. However, when the representatives from the parish met me, they weren't so sure. Fair enough. I am an acquired taste.

Then, I was invited to consider a post in a South Yorkshire mining village. As a result of pit closures and strikes, it was in the process of becoming an ex-mining village. The bishop invited us for lunch to talk it over. But nothing came of it.

Each time I went to see a possible job, R came with me. But with two small children, getting someone to care for them for the best part of a day was a logistical nightmare. So when the next suggestion came up, a parish over two hours away in Birmingham, R suggested she'd stay at home as this one would probably also come to nothing.

There was something peculiar about the ordinary parish of Bordesley Green: the Queen was its patron. Before I visited the parish, I had to have an interview in London. As Her Majesty wasn't up for seeing me in person, I saw one of her officers at 10 Downing Street. As interviews went, it was all chummy, upper-class and insignificant. I got what I needed: clearance to travel to Birmingham to take a look.

Situated two miles from the city centre, the parish of St Paul's was one of many areas of deprivation in the West Midlands. Like neighbouring communities, it found its place between the arterial roads that channelled large volumes of traffic in and out of the city each day. I met the wardens, Jean and John. We talked as they showed me around the densely populated parish with its mixed housing. I saw inside the bleak, austere 1960s church building with its run-down Victorian hall nearby. Alongside was a modern vicarage, more than suitable for our small family.

There was no interview, only our conversation. This revealed so much more than any list of set questions could have elicited. I felt there was a meeting of hearts and minds.

There was an energetic wildness about this small congregation. They were prepared to consider doing all sorts of daring things despite the uncertainty surrounding their long-term future, or maybe because of this uncertainty. The folk who made up St Paul's were truly representative of the local community. Many were the kind of people I had met on the shop floor at the factory or who attended a school like mine. Something felt right, whatever that means. This could work, I thought.

I drove home optimistic and hopeful to tell R. Having spilt the beans, she was keen to see for herself. So, a week later, we travelled south to meet Jean and John and look around. It was strange and refreshing when we ended the day enjoying marmalade sandwiches with them, in a Paddington Bear sort of way, before speeding home. It wasn't long before the bishop's letter of invitation arrived. Adrian and Becca were going to grow up as Brummies.

While I was reluctant to leave Leeds, as it had gone so well, the prospect of moving on to something new also tapped into my long-standing desire to be somewhere else. I didn't have the same need to escape a sadness or a badness, but those age-old emotions tend to linger once they have taken up residence.

It was a warm June when we moved south in 1986. Grandparents were roped in to help with the children and the logistics of our overnight move. The house that was to become our home was more or less ready for us. On the day, box upon box came in through the front door of our new home faster than we could decide where they should go. Even with rooms full of chaos, we had a strong inkling this would be good for us. I had a hunch we'd be here for 20 years, which would then see our teenagers off to work, university or on dossing trips around the world. Here, Adrian and Becca would become young adults.

Those first few weeks seemed wonderful and endless in the heat of the sun. The children ran and toddled around the ample, safe garden well observed by us in the light, airy house. We started to find our way around our side of the city. I'm always surprised when moving somewhere new how the names of local places sound so alien: Alum Rock, Acocks Green, Digbeth. How did these places end up with such crazy names? Soon, they would become familiar, all with stories to tell, impacting our lives with our assumed and soon-to-be altered beliefs.

I became vicar of St Paul's on the balmy evening of 1 July. It was an exciting affair, tinged with hopeful anticipation, a new start for us northerners. It was also a new start for the local folk who must have wondered who this young, fresh-faced guy was and how well he'd fare in this not-so-comfortable urban neighbourhood. Being 31, I was instituted by the bishop as the youngest vicar in the diocese. In place of the Queen, the Deputy Lord-Lieutenant attended to present me. It was a barmy evening, as well as feeling balmy. The Deputy turned up in full official regalia, dressed in polished buttons, flashy epaulettes and tight trousers. Clutching his sword, he stumbled up the aisle wearing ceremonial spurs. The locals thought this was a hoot in its ridiculousness. Even the bishop, in a gentle manner, took the piss.

I was always ill at ease at formal church events. The ceremonial spurs and flashy epaulettes felt far removed from the humble man of Palestine who had no home or symbols of status. Also, this kind of grandeur wouldn't have helped my atheist, agnostic and sceptical friends view my beliefs any more favourably. Thankfully, they wouldn't witness this extravaganza.

The service went according to plan but ended on a ludicrous note. As per tradition, the bishop departed first from the ceremony, followed by the local clergy, dressed in their finest attire. As the new vicar, I was to leave last, energized and eager.

As the visiting organist started up, the bishop departed as planned. The local clergy, seated on one side, began to move, and I positioned myself on the centre aisle's step to bring up the rear. I didn't anticipate that many of the visitors, who were High Church men, would want to genuflect and bow towards the altar as they exited. Unfortunately, I was in their way. As a result, the visiting clergy bowed to me as they left. I couldn't help but smile at the irony of the situation.

It reminded me of the Bible story of Joseph and his brothers I'd learnt all those years ago as a child. Joseph's brothers unwittingly bowed down to him as he ruled over them. Would I one day rule over these men? Well, yes, I would at some point, sort of.

After the service, eager volunteers passed around sandwiches, cakes and tea. My family, including my grandfather, was present; four generations of Turners united in solidarity. Friends from Leeds even came in a coach to bid me farewell. Local dignitaries, head teachers, councillors and others also came to offer their good wishes and departed as soon as possible.

These events were so religious in their earnestness, making it difficult for me to connect with my non-religious, non-Christian friends and associates. But as these jamborees would be infrequent, I knew I had to learn to live with this sort of institutional absurdity whenever it occurred.

There is so much else we do that misleads, confuses and turns away many I care about. As I reflected on this strange yet uplifting evening, I found myself contemplating how I might deal with my struggle of embarrassment within this community, a community unknown to most people beyond the second city.

3 5

Religious fervour

We soon discovered that folk on our side of the city called each other "Bab". This wasn't just when they were talking to babies, but even when addressing grown men and women, bus drivers, police officers, older people, young people, people you knew well and people you didn't know from Adam. This simple tag was a marvellous equalizer; there was no point being pompous about religion. No matter how holy or spiritual you might think you were, you were still "Bab".

Those from my childhood church would have called many of the folk from St Paul's "sinners". This is because they committed the three major "S" sins of smoking, swearing and sex (that is sex while not married). This was a common judgement middle-class Christians made about working-class people in those days. Despite this, I felt comfortable among my new people; they were the sort of people I had grown up with outside of church.

If I couldn't make this Christian business meaningful to them, then there was little prospect of it being genuinely meaningful to me. I was young, I was enthusiastic and somewhat conceited. This was my chance to show how "church" should really be done. I was going to give it my best shot. With R, I would change the world, starting in our little-known neighbourhood of Bordesley Green.

My first job was to sack the organist. Over the years, I'd had to put up with musicians whose playing was so slow that life ebbed out of the congregation as they attempted to sing along. The church council at St Paul's were of one mind; his playing wasn't slow: it was glacial. He had to go. I like others to like me, but sometimes you have to upset one person to please the many. I can handle conflict, although I'd prefer not to deal with it during my first week of a job.

On Tuesday evening, when he came to rehearse his music for the forthcoming Sunday, I climbed the stairs of the organ loft to see him. I sweetened the pill as best I could. Yes, the council had appreciated what he had done over the previous three years. Yes, he could still keep the church door key and come and practise whenever he wanted. Yes, I was sorry for him. But no, he wouldn't be required. He knew he was slow, poor man. He was slow in demeanour and speech too.

At least I felt I had dealt something of a blow to that popular stereotype of church music being dull and unappealing. Organ music isn't the genre of choice for most people, yet for some reason, we've allowed it to take centre stage in the church and remain there for centuries. Most of what is heard Sunday by Sunday isn't even the best experience of organ music. This only serves to confirm people's misgivings about our culture of religiosity. At least this time, when I sacked the slow man, I didn't vandalize the instrument by slashing its bellows!

In those days, I thought how we presented the Jesus message was the reason why new people didn't attend church. If we improved this, I believed the attendance, which averaged around 40 on a good Sunday, would increase.

Getting churchgoers excited about religious things wasn't difficult. Enthusiasm appeals to many and feels much more life-giving than its opposite, apathy. However, religious fervour is a double-edged sword. While it has the power to accomplish great things that older hearts may never achieve, it can also be vain and destroy even the best of intentions.

I was still riding high on the visit to Britain of the Californian preacher, John Wimber. In my new post, I met others who were also keen to try and heal the sick, albeit in a religious manner. This so-called Christian healing created a good deal of excitement on the east side of Birmingham and among numerous churches nationwide. An increasing number of high-profile clergy were saying that this was the "right" thing to do. They saw this as the answer to the church's cultural marginalization. My hope grew. Perhaps this would help relieve my unease about my faith. Perhaps the dramatic and even miraculous would win over those I loved and cared about who couldn't accept what I believed.

The great benefit of this healing model was that any "Bab" could have a go. It didn't depend upon a tremendous charismatic (ego-driven) figure. It was a real leveller. If someone was ill, anyone could pray for them in a simple yet prescribed manner. The unofficial motto of the movement was, "The church is the learning place for the marketplace." We planned to learn how to do this to each other, and then we'd have the courage to go off the well-beaten path to bring healing to the people of Birmingham with our Jesus-style praying. There was a growing mood of optimism and hope within our small, inconsequential congregation. We heard reports of other church communities riding the same wave of fervour. Some people reported they'd found this healing movement helpful, having recovered from various conditions. Whether these were true or not is another matter, but at least those who suffered felt they received some attention. Was God in this? Well, there was something good about it.

Peter, the vicar from the neighbouring parish, was also caught up in the same excitement. We egged each other on, believing this to be the answer to the decline the church faced. Its unsustainability would be a thing of the past. I also entertained the idea that my embarrassment would be a thing of the past. However, when we are young, we often fail to recognize the extent of our lack of wisdom and judgement.

As we spoke to local people who were unwell, they told us their personal stories. But we weren't prepared for what we heard. So many were traumatized. They told us about the terrible sexual abuse and domestic violence they had suffered long before our national institutions started to acknowledge it. I had never been taught about this at college. None of my superiors ever advised me about this. R and I were naïve, even though a young man training to be a vicar had tried interfering with me at a major Christian camping holiday when I was seven. I had buried my memory of that summer and certainly hadn't labelled it as sexual abuse. I just knew it didn't feel right. Safeguarding wasn't on the horizon.

Faced with a deluge of atrocious and disturbing stories, I insensitively assured them, "God can sort this out and heal you!" Some, I am sure, found a degree of comfort. I fear that many others were, in the long term, let down by my sanctimonious words and left in an even worse state than before. I shudder when I recall this.

Like many others, we revelled in these wild and heady days. Many a good story was told, and many a sad story wasn't. Spinning the news is nothing new. It was as if we felt some responsibility for God's reputation; we acted like we were God's public relations team. It took me a while to realize the truth: if God is God, then God can look after Godself.

Looking back, it's clear that our religious enthusiasm had a certain fantastical feel about it. We began talking about acting supernaturally.

I didn't know what I was talking about when using such language. I couldn't help my congregation think more intelligently about the religious language we were caught up in. When we talk about things we don't understand, we often mix in hearsay, folklore and superstitions, which then easily becomes nonsense. This only confirms the suspicions of my atheist, agnostic and sceptical friends, causing them to roll their eyes and sigh.

Through all of this, with the good and despite the bad, I still sensed that awareness of life I'd known years earlier. I'm not talking about religious experience. (I don't think there is anything specifically religious about certain parts of life; there is only Life.) If I had to name it, I would say I had a greater sense of being more profoundly human and connected in these moments. I liked it. While many prefer to express their feelings using religious language, I find it unnecessary and often unhelpful. No one can use the word "God" without some attached assumptions. None of us has travelled through an entirely secular landscape of life. Giving names to our significant experiences in life is an important work as it starts to clarify what we believe and value. But, as I well knew, such talk easily becomes religious gobbledegook.

3 6

Changing the world

Fortunately, we weren't given over completely to excitable religious zeal; we also wanted to do something practical to make a difference locally. Bordesley Green faced numerous challenges, including high unemployment rates, low educational attainment, a lack of community spirit, disillusioned youth, and many dysfunctional families. We wanted to do something about this and believed that God would have us do this because it was the sort of thing the man from Nazareth addressed. However, our congregation faced challenges of its own. We had not been paying our way for many years. We couldn't even afford to update my name, as the new vicar, on the notice board. There was no surplus in the bank account and we owed money to the diocese.

The buildings were also a liability. In 1968, a new church building was imposed on the parish. One local, Gladys, who never wanted it, said, "The vicar told us, 'The architect knows best.'" Locals were not allowed any input. From the time of its inception, the building was never much liked. A chapel in France, designed by the modernist architect Le Corbusier, inspired its design. Its grandeur dominated the landscape and became a burden to the congregation's life. Being powered by electricity, it was too expensive to heat in the winter. It was also inflexible and had an acoustic problem that distorted music and speech.

The original Victorian building, converted into the parish hall, was run down and overshadowed by the new building. Given these circumstances, what could we do?

The people of St Paul's had their reasons for wanting to do something practical about the issues of our local community. They were from the neighbourhood. They, too, had suffered the harsh realities of living in a deprived area. But for me, the wound from my age-old embarrassment about Christianity being too otherworldly lodged in my psyche, and fuelled a desire to make a tangible difference.

As a church community, we argued, scratched our heads, researched, prayed, angsted and spoke to local stakeholders about the issues of our neighbourhood. Although we could not afford to change the vicar's name on the notice board, the church's council decided to undertake a million-pound development project to help bring transformation to Bordesley Green. The decision was unanimous. No one on the committee hesitated, no one blinked. I loved it. These were my sort of people; these were my people.

The decision to embark on this caused some of us to have many sleepless nights over the years that followed. At the time, our project was the most extensive community development initiative in the diocese. We created more than 40 jobs in activities such as a community café, an employment advice centre, a 55-place day nursery, a conference facility, youth projects, an association for refugees, family support activities and a base for local charities. At times, it seemed we had taken on more than we could manage, but we were young. This was another layer of excitement.

Our unusable buildings were refurbished and repurposed, and we acquired an extra property, a shop with a small warehouse. Over time, our little congregation, once marginalized, became a significant player in the community. All this happened as an increasing number of our congregation moved further out of town with the "white flight". The Sunday congregation became smaller and the neighbourhood became more Asian and Muslim over time.

This congregation went above and beyond to serve others. It exceeded the brief of one Mancunian bishop, William Temple, who was reputed to have said in the 1920s, "The Church is the only institution that exists for the benefit of those who are not its members."

I was now more at ease than I'd ever been as a clergyman. I was less embarrassed being a Christian as we demonstrated that being a God-follower wasn't primarily about what happened in religious buildings and meetings. Locals saw what faith in action looked like.

But success can do dark and strange things to you. A few years earlier, I had been a typical young vicar heading up a parish that bobbed along the bottom of the unwritten charts of effectiveness. The high accolades went to the flashy churches in the city's more affluent neighbourhoods. They could count the number who attended their services in their hundreds. But now, when others asked how many came each week to church, I'd reply, "About one and a half thousand, but only 20 on a Sunday morning." Everything we did was "church". My embarrassment couldn't gain traction or energy from this sort of Christianity. I felt I was getting somewhere; this is what faith should look like to non-members.

It is sobering, though, how success inflates the ego. Success always feels good as nobody wants to fail. If something is working, it's natural to want to do more of it. Then, too easily, it can become an obsession, even an addiction.

One day, I was reminded of how I used to feel when I had little success to show for my efforts. With all our initiatives up and running, I had become the head of one of the largest employers in the diocese. I also became the area dean, supervising almost twenty clergy and their parishes. (So yes, harking back to the wonderful absurdity of my institution service, I had started to rule over my colleagues in some sort of way.)

During a monthly chapter meeting, one of my clergy colleagues said, "Graham, you don't realize how threatening all your activities are to the rest of us." I used to know what that felt like, but I had forgotten. If anything, I had become judgemental of others: why couldn't they get on and do something similar? An inflated sense of ego is never attractive to others. Eventually, I would have to learn what happens when one takes the ego too seriously. I would learn how painful it is.

3 7

Unworkable prayer

By the time I was 25, I'd heard plenty of talks on prayer and read more than enough books on the topic. Many, older in the faith, stressed how important it was. Yet nobody ever taught me *how* to pray beyond simply reciting words.

When I knew I would soon be a father, I saw how my brother-in-law, Pete, enjoyed and played with his children, my nephew and niece. He was so good with them; he inspired me. It seemed like fun; I believed I could do the same when our children came along.

But, when I saw others praying, I didn't look and think I wanted to do it the way they did. To be honest, it looked boring. Much of it focused on getting God to do things for us or informing God of what we thought God needed to know. It wasn't unusual that some Christians were regarded as more spiritual than others by how they prayed. I didn't want to engage in this type of one-upmanship or get involved in long and wordy prayer meetings that seemed, most of the time, to be asking God to do things. None of my significant human relationships operated anything like that.

As a teenager, I was encouraged to keep a record of the requests I made in my prayers and list all the ones God answered. My Sunday Bible class teacher told me I would be encouraged by seeing all that God did for me. Even when I was young, I figured out this was vending machine religion which turned God into a commodity provider. If it was possible to relate to God, then there must be more to prayer than this crude simplicity.

Before I retired, I overheard two Christians at work discussing an upcoming holiday. The one due to go on leave said the weather forecast for the week wasn't looking too good. His friend berated him, saying, "John, if you want good weather, you need to name it and claim it to make it so. You need to have faith!"

This reminded me of when I'd heard people pray for favourable weather for an outdoor occasion such as a picnic or an outing. When I expressed scepticism about this, as nearby farmers might require rain for their crops, I was told that God could make it rain on one side of the road and not the other. This made me wonder what sort of image of God or reality was being relied on here. On what assumptions regarding prayer was this based? Whatever they are, they are not understandings I can live with.

It is no wonder some of my atheist, agnostic and sceptical friends like to follow the Australian comedian Tim Minchin. In his *Thank You God* routine, he cleverly and cruelly satirizes this coin-slot approach to prayer. He points out that if God is concerned with dealing with our minor ailments while ignoring children dying from hunger, disease and war in Africa, we have a terrible sort of God. I can't disagree.

Satirists are essential for Christians and religious types. They name what we are not prepared to acknowledge. They expose our shallowness and reveal our blind spots. Unfortunately, many religious folk become defensive and offended when they do this. All of this makes me more inclined to conceal my identity as a Christian and downplay my involvement in the church.

*

Despite all this talk of prayer, I felt I was a hypocrite. I was a vicar who couldn't pray very well. I tried my best I couldn't relate to God as a great cosmic commodity provider. That would never work for me. I worried that the poverty of my prayer would last all my life, as my embarrassment might. My lowest point came when I was sent to a leaders' conference.

I travelled down to Hertfordshire with a colleague in his green Austin Maxi, which had a noisy rear wheel bearing. It summed up our lives; neither of us was in good shape. Deep down, I knew I needed this matter of my hopeless praying to be sorted out once and for all. Exerting my will and having a strict discipline weren't working.

The main conference speaker was the vicar of one of the largest Anglican churches in the country. He was quite a few years older than me. I thought this was typical; we less important guys had to learn from one of the high-performing guys.

His talks were biased towards the upper class, those with posh accents who enjoyed tennis at large country houses, not about people who called each other Bab. I tolerated him.

But his third talk gripped me. It was the story of his struggle with prayer. It was about how he felt he'd failed to fulfil what should have been one of his core tasks as a vicar. After a long ramble about his condition, he said, "So, let me tell you what I do now." He told us that every week, more or less without fail, he prepared some sandwiches and packed a few books and his walking boots before driving out to the countryside. He spent time out there trying to discover how he fit into the world of God, returning home later in the afternoon. As he told his story, a light switched on inside me.

If this could be considered prayer, then I was ready to explore it. Trying to discover my place in the bigger picture of God's reality gave me hope. If he, as the leader of such a large church, could manage this routine, surely I could too. I drove back home with a newfound sense of hope. Maybe even my colleague's car's rear wheel bearing made less noise on our return trip.

I immediately put the plan into action. Each Thursday, I'd get up, make a sandwich lunch, and drive out of town for the day.

How did it go, you may ask? Not very well.

Sutton Park is a nature reserve six miles north of Birmingham. It is one of Europe's largest urban parks and comprises open heathland, woodlands, lakes, wetlands and marshes. This was where I'd hold my weekly appointment with God. It felt strange to have scheduled time when I would try my best to avoid life's many distractions. Regardless of the weather, I visited the park. I was able to walk most weeks. But as I walked, I felt guilty as countless tasks awaited me back in the parish. My day out each week soon started to feel like an indulgence.

Thankfully, my church folk were supportive of my new habit. Some, though, hoped that I'd soon be having profound religious experiences that I'd bring back to share. But most supported my decision without such expectation. In their bones, they recognized there was something human and healthy about this. For me, it was hard to escape the thought that I was being paid to go to Sutton Park to do nothing. It felt like an implicit "Go on then, pray!" was running through my conscience. But nothing changed on that front.

Every week, I made the seven-mile journey through the traffic and charged the mileage to the parish. As I travelled out of town, I'd often listen to talks or lectures by significant Christian thinkers. Once there, I'd walk for a couple of hours. Over the months, I learned most of the paths around the park's 2,500 acres. I developed favourite routes that were less travelled by others. Sometimes I would tire; sometimes I'd feel invigorated. When it didn't seem purposeful, the pointlessness of it all weighed heavily on me. Some days weren't long enough, while others dragged on interminably. I read books I'd intended to read for many years. If I became bored, I'd sometimes listen to the afternoon play on the radio, knowing I had broken one of my self-imposed rules to take time out of life's ordinary activities.

What we call things is important. As clergy, we aren't paid a salary but a stipend. At first, this seems like unnecessary church-speak, but the distinction is crucial. When someone is paid for fulfilling a task or job description, it is called a salary. A stipend is different. Unlike most people in work, I received a payment that allowed me to fulfil my calling without the pressure of meeting targets or producing outcomes. My stipend allowed me first to *be* rather than *do*. Unfortunately, over the decades, this essential distinction has been lost. Many clergy are now as driven as employees in corporations. My stipend meant I could spend one day a week at Sutton Park, enabling me to do what I felt I was ordained for.

I had to learn to let go of my feelings of guilt and understand that turning up and being present was more important than anything else, no matter the result. If I started to think there had to be an outcome, purpose and value would evaporate.

Over the decades of following this discipline, I realized that the best thing I could bring to the experience was my attentiveness. Being present, as best I could, was the only necessary thing. It took me a long time to realize this. But being present isn't easy.

It was like starting to visit a housebound relative I didn't know so well. I wasn't sure what it might do for them, or me. But by keeping our weekly appointments, we grew closer without realizing it and developed a love in the process.

To talk about prayer as love is an excellent way to explore it. Love is not a performance. It is not coercing another to act. It is not about subservience. At its core, it isn't even about saying words.

Love has to be lived in and embraced. It is a longing, a yearning that is fundamental to our existence. We know about this experience of living with our nearest and dearest. It brings us joy and pain, delight and suffering, and despite its downsides, the treasure we wouldn't live without.

I heard that repeating an action enough times can form a habit. My Thursdays became so ingrained that I eventually knew I couldn't do without them. Did my praying improve? I now see that this is not an important question. Did I feel a greater sense of living in the present moment, a greater awareness of living in love? I think so.

3 8

Work smarter

Ongoing success back in the parish continued to be intoxicating. Again, I never expected things to carry on this well. In the buzz of our manic activity, what *weren't* we doing? From the outside, it seemed as if we had the magic touch. The community loved us. The church authorities loved us. The funders loved us. Even we loved us.

Our café on the high street became the preferred venue for workers needing a cooked breakfast, isolated individuals searching for companionship, teachers on their lunch breaks, those attending local training courses and any Tom, Dick or Harriet looking for a bite to eat or a cup of coffee.

The advice centre was the go-to place for any looking for a job, help with a CV, volunteering opportunities and vocational courses. Those up to their ears in debt came for money advice, others to see the MP at his weekly surgery, and some to use the internet. Many were just looking for a friendly face.

Transforming the Victorian hall into a state-of-the-art nursery was a daunting task, almost a bridge too far. Money came in and out of the bank account faster than children and staff came in and out of the front door, making it a nightmare to balance the books. We avoided bankruptcy by the skin of our teeth. In time, it became a thriving business, making us a significant employer in the community.

Despite this success, we still held onto the hope that supernatural healings would change the world and frame our story with fame. I was busy. I was very busy. Taking a day out a week to do nothing in a park seemed like a mad idea and, sadly, it only compounded my workload.

It took me a long time to realize that being "busy" wasn't necessarily good. Often, it is damaging. I recall sitting in Sutton Park when I realized that we often use talk of our busyness to make us appear superior to others. Saying "I am so busy" is meant to impress, and it usually does. There is even a popular saying, "If you want a job done, ask a busy person." Busy people are admired, especially when they can keep it all together.

We were busy doing social justice. We were busy doing everything. We were significant people, keeping it all together (just about).

I found it peculiar that someone stuck at home taking care of elderly parents with dementia or a stay-at-home parent managing three young children never referred to themselves as busy. Even though they worked harder than most of us, their work wasn't considered heroic, so "busy" was never used to describe them. Yet, theirs was hard work, often gruelling.

Years later, during my time in Macclesfield, I noticed that both those working and retirees accepted and valued the idea of being busy. Having experienced the harmful effects of this "busy" mindset, I suggested we stop using this language as it encouraged us to inflate our egos. However, my suggestion wasn't well-received; some even resorted to looking up synonyms in their thesauruses to find an alternative word to use.

I'm not here to judge. In my quest to save the world and demonstrate how to be an effective vicar, I became addicted to busyness as my path to stardom. The saying "work hard, play hard" encapsulated the madness. However, the monk Thomas Merton once claimed that committing ourselves to too many things, too many demands, and trying to help everyone is itself a form of violence—to ourselves and others. I had yet to understand this.

Achieving so much through our small and vulnerable church community was exhilarating. It didn't feel religious, which made me love it even more. However, I soon convinced myself that I needed to be smarter to keep up with the workload. That's when I stumbled upon a diocesan training course I thought could help me. It was a professional time management programme.

For most people, this would cost hundreds of pounds, but we got it for free. It promised to change my attitude toward my work, make me more efficient in using my time and, as a result, more productive. I was eager to enrol. I hoped this would help me overcome my disorganized working practices.

The motivational trainer sold his product well. Although the details of goalsetting and list-making didn't inspire me, his attitude to time did pull me in. Imagine, he said, going to a cashpoint and seeing money spewing from the wall. It would go to waste if you didn't pick it up and spend it. (The fact that, as clergy, we weren't so motivated by money was lost on our energetic trainer.) He followed up by comparing time to the cash machine scenario, emphasizing that if we don't use it, we'll lose it. He persuaded me that time is a valuable resource that shouldn't be squandered.

I returned to the parish with his business package consisting of a diary, filing and planning sheets and a propelling pencil. I was a convert. I was convinced that my life would be different from that point on, and it was. Using what I'd learned, I crammed even more into my days. Now I *was* busy. With my filing system revamped, my time planned and my priorities established, I stumbled less through each day as I had purpose and a method—the corporate method.

I took on new roles and projects. Despite lacking prior experience as a governor, I was appointed the chair of governors for a large local authority school. Along with R, I supported traumatized Bosnian refugees who arrived on our street from the war in Sarajevo. Ensuring that a music charity was introduced into local schools to help support children's self-esteem also became a priority. I brought together ministers of other denominations to hold a neighbourhood festival. I was going great guns. I was on a roll. We were on a roll.

I didn't see what was coming.

3 9

Collapse

I was brought up on a commonly held belief that suggests everything becomes easier if we bravely push on through any struggles or challenges that face us. A parallel religious idea says that expending yourself entirely in service to others is a Godly thing to do. These, though, are not always true.

R and I were doing our bit to save the world, but all of a sudden, she became ill, life-threateningly ill. Concerned friends visited, wanting to help. On Sunday, when it all came to a head, our GP was on call and came to see her. After a short wait, an ambulance arrived. We knew this was serious.

Once R was settled in the hospital on the far side of the city later that day, I came home to Adrian and Becca. Together, we collapsed on our bed and cried. Being hospitalized for six weeks on strong medication, R was taken into what resembled a parallel universe. Our world was turned upside down. We never signed up for this. Would she ever come home the same? The future no longer looked bright and clear but cloudy and uncertain. But with two small children, life couldn't stop: meals had to be cooked, clothes washed, school attended, etc.

Even though these tragedies always wound us, it's remarkable how quickly we adapt to a new situation, despite the background noise of worry and anxiety that remains. R's parents, Mollie and Albert, made regular trips from the northwest to support us. My mother was no longer with us to do the same.

Local folk gave us so much during those difficult days. Many had suffered a similar illness and endured the same treatment. Now, operating as a single-parent father, I continued with my vicar work as best I could. After all, this was all part of the mission I had voluntarily signed up for, wasn't it?

After six weeks, R came home to us, apparently fully restored. There was a new energy and buzz about the house. We took some time off and stayed in a holiday home that was offered to us.

It wasn't long before we picked up our old routines and laughed and sighed as we always had. The storm had passed. (What we didn't bargain for was that the same storm would revisit us a few years later; then, I couldn't believe our bad luck.)

Despite what had happened, we didn't change our pattern of life. We carried on in the same old busy ways, trying to change the world one person at a time. But no one is superhuman. No one is the Archangel Gabriel. We all have our limitations. And I soon came across mine. Overstretched with too much to do, I was still promising to do more than I could deliver. My sleep deteriorated, I became irritable, and the fun of life ebbed away. Rest no longer refreshed me. I felt trapped in a spiral of exhaustion.

One Monday morning, I realized I couldn't continue any more. Depleted and burned out, I stumbled downstairs after another sleepless night and said to R, "I can't do it any more." The words were both a blow and a relief. A blow because I had failed while others I worked alongside pressed on. A relief because I could stop. I made one last trip to town and bought some new speakers for the lounge from Richer Sounds. Then, I lay on the sofa listening to music, staring out of the window, feeling wired and numb. Pink Floyd's lyric rattled around the room, "There's someone in my head, and it's not me." I didn't feel happy or sad, more a sense of confusion and disorientation. My friends and colleagues were incredibly supportive; perhaps they'd seen it coming. Adrian and Becca were magnificent in their gentleness and young concern. R was a great protector of our privacy and the remnants of my sanity in our rather public home at the vicarage. Others pulled to and covered my work for me.

Once I had become accustomed to the blow of not living up to my rhetoric of coping, I felt grateful that the speeding roundabout of life had thrown me off onto stationary ground. The old mantra of "just keep going" was no longer a viable option.

After a week, I started to read. Ploughing through the memoirs of John McCarthy, Brian Keenan and Terry Waite, the Beirut hostages, I wondered whether I was trying to find my path to freedom. Was I starting to realize that the freedom I thought I had was no freedom at all, but a prison?

The world doesn't tell you what to do when life takes a nosedive. Instead, it keeps on shouting "onwards and upwards". It urges us to do more of the same that landed us in the mess in the first place. To keep doing the same thing over and over again, expecting a different outcome, is a well-known definition of insanity. I had ignored the wellbeing of my inner world. But I didn't know what my inner world was. I didn't know who I was. I had found out what I could *do*, but this is never an adequate substitute for who I might *be*.

Suffering does a wonderful job of redirecting our energy back towards ourselves. Eventually, as my world shrank around me, my mind became clearer and more focused. As I observed my present impotence, the past and the future became distant. Spending time in the cocoon of our lounge didn't just provide a safe sanctuary for me; it created some space to look. But I didn't know what I was looking for. Things had fallen apart around me; I had no idea how to put them back together again. It was a Humpty Dumpty sort of moment. All I knew was that I didn't want to come back here again.

Some might say, rather piously, it is only in the darkness that you can see the light. I prefer the more graphic insight that any mother knows: there's always shit before a birth.

4 0

Crisis

My in-laws were good people, faithful through and through. We knew the benefit of their love. They were also solid Church of England types who were pleased and proud to have a vicar as a son-in-law. I think Albert had some reservations about my unorthodox approach; I didn't always do things the Anglican way. He never mentioned it, but I sensed it.

He sent me his past copies of the *Church Times*, perhaps to encourage me not to stray too far from the traditional path. The *Church Times* is the unofficial newspaper of the Church of England. I never bought any copies of my own as there's too much in it that gives energy to my awkwardness and embarrassment, such as bishops in their gold-braided robes looking all episcopal at some prestigious event where everyone defers to them. Additionally, it often features stories of clergy being buffoons by doing something idiotic and often wimpish. This is just the sort of nonsense that tarnishes the rest of us clergy with the same idiotic brush. While, at times, it includes some good articles, it has never been my favourite read.

One edition, though, contained treasure. During my time off work, I flicked through some old issues; I guess looking at the classified ads to see if I could find a less demanding job. At the bottom of one page, I came across a small article about a Franciscan priest who had come over from the USA to speak about Masculine Spirituality. I was intrigued, as I've always been concerned that so few men engage with the church. My concern was, of course, fuelled by my experience at school and my background in engineering. Despite my years-long search for a satisfactory explanation, I only found practical suggestions like creating networks to keep men connected, developing programmes to make them feel more at home in the church and promoting a more masculine culture in church activities and worship. None of these solutions, however, seemed to address the nub of the matter.

The article about the visiting Franciscan had a different ring to it. It talked about the lack of wisdom passed down the generations between men, that left them lost and uncertain. This sounded different. The end of the report stated that I could buy two cassette tapes of the talks for just five pounds. I put my cheque in the post and waited.

When the package came, I powered up my old cassette player and, as soon as Fr Richard Rohr began speaking, I sensed I was about to hear what I so much needed. "Brothers, I am going to give you what I have worked on for some years. I don't know if it is right, but I have given it to many groups, and they seemed to find meaning in it. It is what I call the 'classic spiritual journey of the male.'" As a speaker, Rohr was tentative; I liked that. He also drew on the rich traditions of our heritage, which gave me confidence.

As I listened to the first talk, I could have kicked myself. It was as if I already knew this, while, at the same time, I didn't know it—not in a deep, heartfelt way.

The young man's journey into life, he said, has to begin with a desire to be a hero, to make an impact. He wants to feel significant, and important. He wants to be strong enough to make his mark. I knew this was true for me. When our form teacher at secondary school asked each of us what we wanted to be when we grew up, I said, "A pilot". The teacher no doubt rolled his eyes and moved on to the next hopeless case. But we accept this of boys; we are pleased they have aspirations. Rohr said this is wonderful for the first half of life; it is a pity when people are still trying to be heroes in their fifties. At some point in life, there will be, for most, an experience of uncertainty, crisis or pain. We laugh and call it the mid-life crisis. Rohr called it the Great Defeat. An event will happen, he said, that you won't expect: an experience of suffering, a feeling of being out of control, seemingly unable to do anything about it. It might be a major crisis or illness. We may wake up one morning and say, "Is this all there is?" The Christian tradition calls this the Dark Night of the Soul. It was nothing new, although it was for me.

As I listened to his voice, I remembered the only preacher from college who had left a lasting impression on me, Bishop Michael Marshall. Hadn't he told us about his pain, failure and suffering? Didn't he tell us how we had to learn how to transform our wounds into something that was love-filled and redemptive? I recalled leaving that service believing that I, too, might face some struggles. I expected it to happen when I started in Leeds. But it didn't. As a result, I had forgotten his warning.

Through the nuggets of wisdom on these two tapes, I discovered that I had been led to a place where I couldn't fix, control or understand life. This was painful, but it was gold, even more precious than gold.

Rohr continued. We can make many responses to such a crisis, but only one leads to wholeness. It is the downward journey from the cleverly protected ego-self into reality. The ego is not *who* I am. It is only who I and others *think* I am. It's not necessarily bad; it's just not the real deal. Who I am is much deeper and more wonderful. Who I am consists of love.

In my collapse, it felt as if something within me had died. I realized I wasn't as great as I thought I was. In free fall, I looked for some handholds to steady me and I hoped this wisdom might be the answer.

As Christians, we talk a lot about dying; it is central to all we hold dear. However, we consign such talk to the annals of history, restricted to an event long before our time, the death of the carpenter-messiah on a hillside outside the contested city of Jerusalem.

My experience wasn't unique. Others have also known a frightening descent into apparent oblivion. Gary Barlow (of Take That fame) expressed this when his second album tanked following the success of his first. "I felt I was dying," was his comment. He felt he had become a non-entity. For many, it is not always so dramatic. Some simply feel life no longer makes sense or has any purpose.

I was never taught about the significance of "dying, while still alive" during my Christian upbringing. Instead, the emphasis was always on striving for continual improvement, the onwards and upwards game— the message widely promoted in the world. Many churches today still follow this impulse, as expressed in their many straplines and slogans about growth. I was never taught about the importance of dying to my ego. This message doesn't pull in the crowds or fill the pews for a Sunday morning service. Jesus referred to it as the narrow way.

After listening to Rohr's talks, I was left stunned. How did I not know this? But to go into a self-questioning rampage is to return to the old habit of trying to understand everything. I knew I had to learn to live and be different, to discover the life I already had but didn't recognize. I knew I needed to learn to live without being so attached to my ego, but I wasn't sure how. Being humbled by my disintegration was a help along the way.

I now had to discover where this would lead me.

4 1

Disorientation

Something had changed. If you asked me what it was, I couldn't say. I was cautious about getting back to work after six weeks out of action. My colleagues gave me that concerned look as if I might suddenly do or say something irrational or disturbing. I understood their apprehension. When someone returns from a collapse or breakdown, you're never too sure how deep their journey into darkness has been. It isn't a sorrow you can glibly enquire about, unlike a more straightforward matter, such as a broken leg or appendicitis. These can even be joked about. But we don't joke about these weightier matters, and rightly so.

As I emerged, it seemed as if the landscape had shifted. I felt altered. I knew I couldn't go back and that was a good thing. But I didn't know what lay ahead; that was disorientating.

This disorientation taught me that we don't see things as they are; we see them as we are. This wasn't a profound thought of mine; others had discovered the same. But it was a critical turning point for me. I had devoted so much of my life to bringing change to the world that I had never understood how I needed to change.

Throughout my Christian upbringing, I never received a clear explanation of how the process of transformation in a person happens. Perhaps I'd misunderstood it, but what I heard was: accept that you have gone wrong in life, believe in Jesus, have faith in God, and try to be good.

Being good is an impossible task. I now know I'm not alone in feeling this way. For much of my life, I assumed I must be weak-willed. Other Christians made it appear easy to behave and spread the word of Jesus. But I couldn't. I couldn't *not* be embarrassed about being a "Jesus freak". I couldn't shake off my disquiet when everyone else seemingly didn't have my qualms. So it was an enormous relief for me, and a boost to my flagging hope, when I remembered that the great St Paul (hero of the church and writer of big chunks of the Bible) struggled to do the right thing. In his despair, he admitted to doing the wrong things instead of the right things he knew he should be doing. I wish I knew what those bad things were— we could've compared notes.

As I battled with my inner turmoil, I realized that our faith had become focused on "doing right things". Every religion has done this in one way or another. Maybe this is why many have ditched their religion to seek something better. The truth of the matter is that we are all broken. I now knew I was broken.

When I lead groups about such topics, I enjoy playing a song called *All My Favourite People Are Broken* by the band Over the Rhine. The song's lyrics tell us we are all part saint and part sinner who shouldn't be afraid to admit we're beginners. It's an open song of welcome to "awful believers" and "sceptical dreamers". It is hauntingly accurate.

Those who make out that they aren't broken, but well-behaved, come across as some of the most unattractive people. Jesus found this to be true with those who were religious. I think that's why he preferred to party with the misfits, oddballs, known sinners, awful believers and sceptical dreamers. They knew they weren't okay. That was more than okay with him. Many of my atheist, agnostic and sceptical friends fit into this category. They're also usually good people to laugh or party with. I am convinced that this wildness was the stuff that Jesus couldn't help but be drawn to.

Setting out into life after my season of incarceration, I began to view things from a different perspective. Some Christians emphasize the concept of being "born again". The phrase has been bandied about in terrible and sometimes destructive ways. Many of my non-Christian and non-church friends know that this title often carries an attitude of superiority, even arrogance, about it. These individuals consider themselves to be "proper Christians". They imply they don't live their faith in a half-hearted manner or embarrassingly, as I did. This always grated with me.

Through my collapse, I gained a new understanding of the term "born again". It has nothing to do with a believer's quality, rank or status. It has nothing to do with feeling superior; that's not what Jesus meant. Instead, being born-again is all about starting over again, afresh. Some traditions call it returning to the beginner's mind. It is about looking out on the world and being curious, *as if* for the very first time. No two moments in life are ever the same. No two items are ever identical. If I boil the same kettle for another cup of tea or walk the same route through the woods as the day before, they are different. To be born-again is to become childlike (not childish) once more. It is to start to see differently and to ask "Why?" again and again.

I didn't know it then, but I was starting down a path that many had taken before me—it was called the Contemplative Way.

Through my turmoil, my ongoing embarrassment with faith had, more or less, been forgotten. Holed up in the vicarage, away from the public, gave me a sense of solace from my discomfort. That, too, was a welcome relief. However, the prospect of returning to work and my vicaring duties reminded me that the issue still lingered. Even what I had been through hadn't dislodged it; maybe it was here to stay. Perhaps I'd even have to see this differently.

4 2

The learning quest

Sometimes, life feels like a giant game of Jenga, that tower-building and collapsing woodblock game we get out at Christmas. As we work our way through life, we build our towers of achievements and triumphs, block upon block. It isn't always a bad thing; sometimes it's necessary. Our constructions can reach some giddy heights yet remain stable and secure. But as we all know, life wounds us; we may even lose some of those much-valued blocks of life. We might wobble a bit, but still, everything somehow holds together. Then, when we are least expecting it, a crucial plank of life is ripped from beneath us, and our tower comes tumbling down around us. We then have to start all over again the process of reconstruction.

I had to make sense of the collapse of my tower. What could I do? In my uncomfortable landscape of scattered Jenga blocks, I was still sure of one thing: I did not want to return to how life had been. The prospect of attempting to rebuild the tower of my old life didn't appeal to me in the slightest.

As I surveyed my chaos, I realized I had been brought up on a diet of religious certainty. We were the Christians who had it right. The Bible was clear, and we were following it. All we needed was to have faith. I was told, "Be bold and press on." My college motto, "Be right and persist," was also lodged in my head. Growing up on such a high-octane belief system makes it hard to shed that need for certainty. I had memorized it, lived it intensely, and then taught it to others. Was I hooked on it? Like many of my time, I was thirsty for certitude. I had not yet realized that Jesus never gave people a bulletproof ideology. Loyalty and faithfulness were central for him, for this is the stuff of relationships, not creeds and belief systems.

There were things I knew I must leave behind. The five-pound cassette tapes made me aware that there was a version of life that was so much better. As with many leavings, there was a sense of loss and grief. What would I be without all I had thought necessary? What will I have in place of what I thought was so correct? I hoped that the insights, understandings and experiences I was being introduced to could make more sense to me, as well as to my atheist, agnostic and sceptical friends. I even hoped they would eventually erode the strength and domination of my embarrassment. It would take time, but my intuition was right.

To help keep me grounded, I enrolled on another night class. We had a decent camera with a few interchangeable lenses, so I chose photography.

I travelled three miles out from our Birmingham parish to the class on Monday evenings. The first session at any new class is always a bit stiff and awkward as everyone eyes each other up. Like the car maintenance classes I'd taken, this was very much a bloke's thing.

We brought examples of our work each week and planned what we might do next. What I wanted to learn, though, was how to use the darkroom. In the days before digital photography took off, being able to use a darkroom set you apart as a more serious photographer. The darkroom should have been called a red room really, as all the processing took place to the background glow of a red light. It would have been impossible to do anything in complete darkness.

Locked in this room, sloshing around our film and photographic paper in chemicals, was how we, as students, got to know each other. In time, there would be the inevitable question, "So, what do you do?" But Bob never asked me. He said, "I know who you are."

Bob used to drink at the Adderley Park pub. One of his mates was a heavy drinker, probably an alcoholic. One dark and cold evening, his friend staggered out of the pub, got halfway across the road and collapsed. It was just his misfortune that a wagon came around the corner and killed him. Bob said, "You took his funeral. I remember you. You did all right." He was still much affected two years on. We stood in silence in the glow of the light until he told me how the horror of his friend's death happened.

Bob was just the sort of agnostic that I was drawn to, an ordinary guy. He wasn't perfect, but he wasn't completely bad either. I felt an affinity with him. Over the years, we chatted about many issues while locked in the glimmer of that room. We laughed about much madness, too.

Bob had a finger missing. This wasn't uncommon in Birmingham. The motor industry had been the industrial backbone of the city for decades until it started to wane. Factory safety wasn't what it is today. Fingers were lost in the unguarded machinery, sometimes even an arm. It wasn't unknown for lives to be lost.

I was astonished one Sunday morning when our small congregation came to receive the bread and wine of the communion service. They stood in a circle, holding out their hands. Of the 22 people there, five of them had a finger, or part of a finger, missing. This happened when I started to weary of asking God to make people better. Many like someone to pray for them. I understand that; it is good and positive attention. That, in itself, can be beneficial. But if one of these fingers grew back, that would be a miracle. Of course, no fingers ever did grow back.

It made me all the more aware that I had an inadequate understanding of so many things to do with my faith. My theology was weak and my trust in the "getting God to do things" sort of prayer was not as robust as it once was.

In an attempt to rebuild my life, I started on a grand search. I read avidly and listened to recorded lectures. I spoke to anyone I thought could help me and avoided those I knew couldn't.

I've always needed to understand; this is both a strength and a weakness. It creates an urge to learn, which is good. But for a long time, it was an unrecognized drive and, therefore, had the hallmarks of an addiction. I assumed I could get some control over my life (and a handle on the world) if I understood everything. I harboured the unacknowledged belief that if I had all the certainties the world could offer, my life would be better, even whole. But richness and fulfilment come from a different place.

As I set out on my search, I discovered I was dyslexic. Listening to a random World Service radio programme in the middle of a sleepless night, there was a discussion about people who sounded much like me. They knew they weren't stupid but had struggled with their education. I never read a book until I was 14. I couldn't study or pay attention for long. It always puzzled me that R could sit down to complete a piece of work without the stress and discomfort I experienced. She said it was simple; you just need to answer the question. But it had never been so simple for me.

At diocesan and governing body meetings, I was often foxed when I couldn't digest the contents of a discussion paper passed around as we started the agenda. Sitting alongside my colleagues, my mind was distracted by everyone and everything else in the room. I couldn't concentrate as others did. Why not? Well, now I might know.

Through our advice centre, I tracked down someone who could help me. A few days later, a trip across town for an assessment told me all I needed to know: "You demonstrate most of the indicators associated with dyslexia." The three-page report outlined my preferred learning styles, my problems with sequencing and how I might best be helped. The fact that I had a "condition" was great news. My struggle with education had been explained. I may have been a bad boy at school, but that wasn't my only problem.

Armed with my report, printed on yellow paper, I set out with even more energy on my learning quest. I was on a mission to discover what I had missed and find out what could help me move forward after a series of backward steps.

4 3

No longer Christian

One day, as I was driving to the supermarket, Becca asked from the back seat of the car, "Daddy, are there more brown people in our country than white people?" She was nine. It wasn't a resentful enquiry but an innocent question. One of my favourite photographs from that time is of Becca with her four best friends. One was Indian, one mixed-race Arab, one mixed-race African-Caribbean and one blonde European. They are all smiles. This, we know, is how life should be.

Most of our neighbours were Muslim; their families originated from Pakistan. The Bosnians who moved in over the road were secular Muslims. Many religious traditions were represented among our staff team, including Hindus, Sikhs, Rastafarians, Muslims, Christians of different denominations and, of course, atheists, agnostics and sceptics. It was a great mix. Faith was never a problem.

There was an acceptance and ease whenever anyone mentioned God. There wasn't the embarrassment of God-talk that I felt during my school and factory days. What everyone meant by this touchstone word was, of course, another matter. I loved this ease of relating.

There was, however, a dark side to this religious mix. We all identified with a label, a description, a religion. While there was never an issue among friends and work colleagues, there was sometimes conflict in the community.

There were two main cultural groups. There was the residual white community, many looking to move further out of town. If they identified as anything, it would be vaguely Christian or nothing. The growing community in the neighbourhood was Muslim, which during our time became the majority.

Within sections of the residual population, there was a mood of resentment. "These Muslims are taking over," was the complaint. The Muslim community, on the other hand, was often defensive in the face of this hostility. But then, that strange thing happened when dissimilar groups rubbed up against each other. Families and individuals could be racist towards those they didn't know, but often the Muslims who lived next door to them were "lovely". True encounter between people changes us.

In the middle of this community dynamic, I was a Christian living among Muslims. As I tried to find a new orientation in life following my disintegration, I became increasingly uncomfortable with my label. It only served to reinforce that my tribal allegiance was different to my neighbour's. How did that serve the common good of a humanity made in the image of God? As I thought about this, I remembered the line fed to me so many times over the years, "Jesus did not come to create a new religion." But that is exactly what my faith community had turned our tradition into. Our religion was Christianity. We were Christians.

Jesus never talked about Christianity. Neither did St Paul. They weren't Christians; they were Jews. The term "Christian" is hardly ever used in the Bible and only once by the faith community itself. The title of Archbishop Desmond Tutu's book puts it bluntly: *God is not a Christian.* The word "Christianity" never appears in the Bible.

So, I decided to stop using these labels, if at all possible. I didn't want or need a tribal affiliation. I was no longer a Christian. If I was a member of anything religious, I was a member of the global church. This is what my baptism was about. If I had to have a label, it would be "someone trying to follow Jesus".

Tribal affiliations and identifications with ideologies, religious or not, have torn our world community apart and caused division within and between nations. The damage I had done by my attachment to my ego was bad enough. But in world history, we know what the devastating collisions of collective egos looks like. Despite the harm that has been done, we are nonetheless gravely attached, even addicted, to our labels and egos, both individual and collective. I didn't need to describe myself as a Christian any longer. I was a follower of Jesus; I belonged to the church—that was all I needed. When I consider the damage done and the negative attitudes I've encountered over the years, I wonder if the term "Christian" has even become toxic.

Still, today, people don't believe that I haven't called myself a Christian for over 25 years. As I no longer have to protect the brand, I feel freer.

The unnecessary division between me and others has been reduced, something that feels closer to the ethos of Jesus.

The outrageous preacher/pastor Nadia Bolz-Weber was once pulled up by one of her friends, who said, "Every time we draw a line between us and others, Jesus is always on the other side of it." I resolved to stop drawing lines wherever I could. After all, the great master did tell us numerous times not to judge.

4 4

Staff Team Day

Once a year, we held a Team Day for everyone we employed and those who volunteered with us. This was to help nurture a sense of community, share the vision of what we were about and give us a chance to let those we worked with know how much we appreciated them.

These days had been okay in previous years, but only "okay". We were struggling to find a theme that was engaging. While worthy, reviewing our mission statement and values was never very inspiring.

One year, we racked our brains to think how we could do it better. After a great deal of scratching our heads, we decided to take a risk and base the day on the theme of forgiveness rather than anything related to the specific activities we ran. This was an important value for many of us. However, we didn't want the day to be religious in any way, nor did we want to give the impression that we were attempting to make converts of those who came. It was a risk. We hadn't done anything like this before and we had no idea how it might turn out. I knew management theory was starting to talk much more about forgiveness and other "softer" topics, so it wasn't a completely batty idea.

We arranged the seating in a large circle in our new conference hall for the nearly 50 who attended. As Saturday mornings are not the best time to get people interacting with each other, we started with some warm-up activities. Then, we invited each person to select two stones from a pile in the centre of the room and asked them to keep these until the end of the day. One was to be a "good stone", and the other was a "not-so-good stone". We'd come back to these later.

Following the warm-up, we divided those present into four smaller groups and asked each of them to look back over the past 12 months and write on cards all the things that had happened in the name of St Paul's Crossover, our organization. We encouraged healthy and noisy competition between the groups to help get them motivated. It was important to have a review, as not everything had gone well. As managers, we had made some poor decisions. There was also some sadness when a popular staff member died of cancer shortly after his diagnosis. Because of these, staff morale had taken a knock. We felt that these sad things should be named, owned and even forgiven. There were also plenty of good and positive things to celebrate and laugh about.

At the end of this session, each group brought their cards and laid them on a 12-month timeline we had arranged down the centre of the hall. Jo Bagby, our business manager, talked us through the events that our cards highlighted. We named what had happened.

After a coffee break and a team photograph, we got closer to our chosen theme of forgiveness. I outlined how we all like people who are forgiving, yet we often struggle with forgiving others. At the same time, we don't warm towards hard and bitter people; they repel us. But we like those who forgive, especially if it is us who need to be forgiven.

To make it more personal, we told stories of how we'd messed up. I started. I told the story of a funeral that I had spoiled. When visiting the grieving family, I'd promised to include in the service a poem the deceased had written some years before. When it came to the end of the funeral, the family made their way out of the chapel. This is usually when people thank you for what you've done. It wasn't so this time. The bereaved husband, from his wheelchair, held my hand and said, "So what happened to the poem you promised to read out?" I had forgotten. There was nothing I could do to put it right. I was horrified. The funeral was over. All I could do was apologize. The whole family walked past me looking unhappy; some wouldn't shake my hand. I knew I had spoiled their day.

Jo told of an incident with her five-year-old son. When putting him to bed one night, he asked, "Why didn't you come today, mummy?" Suddenly, Jo remembered that she had promised to go to school to see him receive an achievement award. She had forgotten and was horrified. She knew she needed her son's forgiveness.

John Bleazard, who had been instrumental in starting up most of the activities at St Paul's Crossover, spoke about how we had failed as an organization. We'd set up an after-school club to serve local families. Staff had been recruited, and parents depended on it. Unfortunately, the initiative didn't go well. Soon, the financial losses started to ramp up and we couldn't cover the deficit, so the club had to close. One staff member was made redundant, and parents and children were let down. We, as an organization, also needed to know forgiveness. A sober mood descended on the gathering in our hall.

To follow this up, we sent everyone back into their small groups where they found plenty of card, glue, magazines, candles, sticks and other bits and pieces. They were asked to create something that summed up what forgiveness meant to them. After 40 minutes, they would present their creations to everyone else.

My hunch was that this might not work. The task seemed too vague. But after a few minutes, there was a lot of activity and chatter in each room. Maybe it would be all right.

After three-quarters of an hour, all four groups returned with their creations, each person still carrying their two stones.

The first was a bridge made of card and covered with magazine pictures including people from diverse ethnic groups. For this group, forgiveness was about moving from everything wrong and painful to experiences of reconciliation, harmony and peace.

The second was similar. They had made a series of steps leading from what was bad up to what was good. Negative newspaper headlines and images of suffering were at the bottom of the steps. Going up the steps was a series of improving pictures. At the top step was a lighted candle.

The third was a tunnel. It started at "Cock up" and finished with "We forgive". Around the tunnel were pictures stating the sort of things that go wrong. On top of the tube of the tunnel were phrases such as, "Talk about it," "How do we feel?" and "Learn from what went wrong."

The last presentation was a collage of pictures pasted onto a board. At the centre was a simple image of a cup on which was written, "The cup of forgiveness." When I asked why there was a cup, Dot (who was not a church member) said, "Well when I fall out with someone, I chat with them and then ask them to come round for a cuppa tea." Forgiveness is about drinking together. (In our religiosity, we, as church people, might recognize this as something sacramental.)

These four creations were then placed around the timeline down the centre of the hall. Some photographs of our activities and people we knew were added. The hall floor was covered with our days' work.

For the final session, we invited everyone to do two things. First, they placed their "good stone" alongside something on the floor that they were thankful for and pleased about. After a moment's reflection, we placed our stones around the circle in turn.

Then, I invited people to place their second stone, the "not-so-good stone", by something that symbolized where they had to express forgiveness, be forgiven or even forgive themselves. As we did this, the track *Everybody Hurts* from R.E.M. played in the background. The atmosphere in the room began to change. I started by placing my stone alongside the part of the timeline that struck me. The woman next to me placed hers. Then, one by one, everyone around the room followed suit. As some placed their stones, a few started to cry a little. More stones were placed, but then a few ran out of the room holding tissues. Others were more than keen to place their stones against the image of their choice. The music ended just after the last person placed their second stone. Those who had left the room did not return, and this made me nervous. I was uncertain how well the session had gone.

I ended the day with a poem about hope, and we left to go home. It had been an emotional session. John, Jo and I were unsure how well it had been received. But we shouldn't have been concerned.

Many stories were told the following week about what had happened at the Team Day. Some had managed to forgive themselves for things that had happened years before. Some had managed to pluck up the courage to forgive family members and then go home to reconnect with them. Some were relieved to receive forgiveness. And others had never understood what forgiveness was all about until that day.

Involved in those discussions were people who had a faith, those who had no faith and many who were unsure whether they had a faith or not.

When some of the young Muslim women who worked in our nursery went home to their families clutching tissues, their fathers wanted to know why the church had upset them. But, no, they said they were not upset and they shared their stories.

There was no embarrassment that day. There was no religion. But if you pushed me, I would have to say (using religious language) that there was something of God present, something I still today would call Love, the Great Love.

If I could have bottled the essence of that day, I would have done. It touched what was real. It wasn't complicated, but it was profound. If my calling was to do anything, it was to do this: to help lead people into a deeper experience of life—life in all its fullness.

Through all that had happened to me and around me, I grew less and less interested in the church as an end in itself. What I was experiencing and what we were building in our community felt much more important than simply attempting to make a congregation grow. As the years passed, church culture became even less attractive to me. Also, I had never been an enthusiast of trading in Christian clichés or religious language, but now I was even more committed to eliminating it from my speech. Forgiveness was good, but it must be expressed in down-to-earth, concrete terms. Before I left Birmingham, something happened that made me realize once again how important it was to live and speak in straightforward and unsanctimonious ways.

4 5

Jack

A call one day from an undertaker sounded more serious than usual. Could I take the service of a 31-year-old who had been murdered? Yes, of course, I would. I rearranged my diary and left to visit Jack's parents.

There was no way to describe the atmosphere in the home of these two tender, devastated people. Their only son, aged just 31, had been battered to death in a brutal homophobic attack. There is no benefit in recounting here what the murderer did to his body, but it was worse than most people could imagine.

Jack was a gifted artist and a highly regarded college lecturer. He was close to his parents and well-integrated into the gay community of Birmingham. His brutal death was not only a great injury to Jack and his family but also to his wider community. They, too, were devastated, but they had also become scared.

I sat with his parents in their home, not having the first idea of what it might be like to lose a child, let alone your only child, due to a callous murder. It is hard to describe how humbling it is to sit with people in such deep pain. It is a sobering honour few experience.

As I sat with them, I couldn't be anything but attentive. I said little beyond, "Do you want to tell me about it?" They kept returning to what had happened as if to discover what they could verbalize and what they couldn't. It is said that the best things in life cannot be spoken about. But neither can the worst. I met with them several times in the fortnight before the funeral. Every time I called to see them, there was something wonderful in their presence, along with the terrible horror.

It reminded me of other tragic deaths I'd encountered. There is something about such grief and loss and pain that draws people into an egoless present. Honesty and humility can no longer hide behind well-crafted defences and images fashioned over the years. Like many, I'm drawn to these situations, but not because I am ghoulish. I'm drawn because in the present moment of these terrible events is a naked expression of life found in few other places. It all feels so real. We all want a bit of what is real, but such reality comes at a price. Grief is an expression of love. Many, including the late Queen, have quoted the line, "Grief is the price we pay for love."

The funeral took place just beyond the city boundary in a modern crematorium chapel. When I arrived, a large number of young adults had already gathered. It made my heart pound; I knew I had an important and sensitive job to do. I wanted to do my best for their sake.

As Jack's parents arrived in the limousine, following the hearse, the silence of the moment was heavy with meaning.

I cannot remember much about the service, but I can remember it felt intense. It was a grander expression of what I felt at his parents' home. There was a deep awareness. No one was distracted by the frivolities of life. We all connected with those who felt Jack's loss the most. We connected with the shock of what had happened and the evil that had been done.

I don't care what people call that sense of presence, whether they name it Love, God, consciousness or reality. We spend too long imprisoning our experiences with these words; we rob them of their beauty, wonder and even horror. We strip them of their mystery. Life is too short to argue from our fixated minds what to label them.

Because of all that had happened, I knew I wanted to spend more time experiencing life in its rich fullness. I also knew I wanted to help others know the same.

That rich fullness was also present at the memorial service we held a few weeks later.

Jack's family and friends from the gay community filled St Paul's Church with colour, life and vitality. There was an exhibition of his work. Two strong feelings ran intertwined throughout the service: utter grief and heartfelt gratitude. Stories were told, silences shared, tears shed, and Jack celebrated.

Most clergy say they prefer to take a funeral or a memorial service rather than a wedding, as they contain so much that we all hunger after. Only by being immersed in such encounters over the decades could I understand that crazy-sounding saying of Jesus, "Blessed are those who mourn." This was something bigger than religion.

4 6

Presence

As I continued stumbling my way through life, I became aware that what was happening to me was changing me more than I could ever have expected. My chronic embarrassment with faith couldn't get any traction when I passed through these moments of great intensity. This gave me hope.

I remembered how I could enter into profound experiences of presence as a child. In the years before I entered secondary school, I used to lie flat on my bed and close my eyes. As I tried to feel the stillness of my arms and legs and body, I would get a sensation of floating off the bed. It felt good to me. I didn't know what it was all about and still don't. But looking back, I knew I was very much in the present moment. I felt alive to myself.

It even happened at school. During the daily assembly, we'd stand to sing a hymn. This would be followed by a prayer, for which we'd remain standing. We were told to close our eyes. As I stood there, I would get the sensation again of rising and floating, as if the portion of the floor I was standing on was coming up with me. After some moments, I would feel so far up that I became fearful of falling. This caused me to stagger sideways and open my eyes, which is when the beauty of the moment was lost.

Some more cautious, even fearful, believers might say it wasn't a Christian thing to do. Who says, I ask? I now recognize that it was an experience of being in the present moment and a deep connection with reality. I now understand that Love or God or consciousness or reality can only be known in the present moment. I want to experience this aspect of life even more than I want to *know* about it.

Birmingham had given me so much. It had done so much *to* me. Some things had been beyond painful. Because of this mix, I knew I left Bordesley Green quite different to the person I'd been when we arrived. I was now to move on to something quite different.

Adrian went off to university. Becca went to travel the world. And we moved to Macclesfield.

RECTOR

4 7

Macclesfield

On the face of it, I wasn't well qualified to become the rector of Macclesfield. The job was to lead a large town-centre church and oversee three other congregations. Over almost 20 years, my previous congregation fell from 35 or so to an average of just over a dozen; I didn't have much to draw on. Working in a middle-class parish would also be a new experience for me. However, I knew about complex organizations, and St Michael's was complex.

After so long in Birmingham, I was ready for a change. R would have stayed longer if she could, but my time was up. My sell-by date had expired. I'd been working on my exit strategy for a couple of years. Our community businesses in Bordesley Green couldn't just be dropped. Other managers needed to be put in place. My role as the vision-holder had to be passed on to others.

It was odd for me, being embarrassed about being a clergyman, to move to the town centre church of Macclesfield with all its civic and traditional connections. In Birmingham, I'd been able to live lightly with my identity as a Christian and a cleric. Being the rector of Macclesfield was quite a different matter. This was a high-profile public role. I would feature in the town's affairs so couldn't be inconspicuous.

We moved to Macclesfield for several reasons. R's parents were ageing and becoming frail; we felt we should be closer at hand. Their hometown of Widnes was only 40 minutes away.

I also needed to work in a different type of context. A clergy colleague from Birmingham once said to me, "You've probably only got one 'Bordesley Green' in you, if you're honest." It had been a wild and exciting time, but I knew I couldn't do it again. I didn't have it within me.

Along with this, I wanted to be where there was a more established and settled congregation that lived less hand-to-mouth. Macclesfield had many more able and available people to work alongside. As I flourish most when working with others, this attracted me. I also felt that my lack of obvious qualification could be a strength, not just a weakness. It is often the outsider, even an apparently ill-equipped person, who can see what others cannot see.

The move was a risk, I knew that. But I can cope better with risk than boredom. I was about to enter what I did not know.

*

The imposing building of St Michael's stood tall and bold next to the town hall's Greek-styled columns. It had all the obvious religious trappings of a long-established ecclesiastical institution with well-renowned stained glass, large bell tower, robed choir, pipe organ and seating for hundreds in its nave. Its dark, ancient Gothic chapel (with the frightening name, the Savage Chapel) made regulars and visitors alike regard this as a "proper church".

A recent major refurbishment and creative redesign of the rear of the building convinced me that there was energy and vision in this congregation. It indicated that they wanted a different future from what had been their past. But still, this role would test my battle with the discomfort of all things churchy that haunted me.

Even though I was now in a different place from where I was 20 years earlier, the echoes of that nagging tone still prevailed. The parental voice within me still told me to forget my dis-ease and get over my awkwardness. Maybe it would be in Macclesfield that I'd come to peace with it all and learn to live an unembarrassed life. There wasn't, though, any way that I wanted my atheist, agnostic and sceptical friends to see what I was getting myself into.

The problem with any well-established and successful institution is that it has an unwritten and unspoken value: survival. St Michael's was no different; there was an underlying desire to "keep things going". Among some was the anxiety that the church, or some of its activities, might in time collapse and be lost. For these, there was the expectation that my job was to run the church and get more people into its services.

It is hard to be part of something that no longer looks as strong or significant as it used to. Those I had left behind in Bordesley Green knew a lot about this. They were much further down this road and had grown through it. They taught me how to live in it with less anxiety.

Jonathan Sacks (one-time Chief Rabbi) was a master of words and ideas. He insisted that religions are always at their best when they are a minority. But we like to be mainstream. Sadly, "main" often means dominant.

Fortunately, enough folk in St Michael's and many from across the other three churches didn't want to be dominant. They wanted to serve the town, think afresh about what they believed, explore spirituality, address global and local issues, and be changed in the process. Because of these wonderful human beings, I said yes to the bishop's invitation and was instituted as the rector at a well-attended service on an April evening in 2005.

The Queen's representative was not required this time, so there were no ceremonial stirrups or flashy epaulettes. Nevertheless, there was still plenty of ceremony and ancient peculiarity, with many of us dressed in out-of-age attire. There was also an air of expectation for a new start. I hoped I could pull it off.

My unease about these events sometimes gets the better of me. It is not difficult for my behaviour to become childish or inappropriate. A few years later, after his retirement, another good friend, David Wightman, was ordained to become an additional minister at St Michael's. He was to focus his energies on the town centre with its shops and businesses.

Ordination services in cathedrals are highly choreographed events. David was one of 20 being ordained that morning. The cathedral was packed. I was one of about 40 clergy ready to process down the aisle following a large choir, lay preachers, acolytes and other sundry folk. We were all dressed up to the nines.

The organ blasted, the congregation sang, and we filed our way down the long nave, looked on by a full cathedral. Partway down, I saw David's wife, Chris, at the end of a row, just to my right. They're a good-humoured couple and always ready for a laugh or a joke. As I approached her, I moved a little out of line to the right so I might brush against her. I knew it would make her smile. Something went a little awry, and I collided with her more than I should have. My right arm bashed her left shoulder, and she lurched forward, shocked and startled. I quickly found my place back in the procession, stifling my need to laugh.

What makes me do this, apart from getting a cheap laugh? It's not unrelated to the embarrassment and the awkwardness I feel about being in such religious situations. I guess I am fearful that this elaborate formality draws me into another world, away from the many non-Christian and non-church people I have an affinity with. Some think my faith is irrelevant and ignore it or treat it with disdain. Some are angry. So, I sometimes mess about to distance myself from what I see as religiosity.

The singer/songwriter, Hozier, wrote an angry song, *Take me to church*. Growing up in County Wicklow, Ireland, he was bitter and lashed out in his music. Frustrated with the church, recoiling from a broken relationship and trying to express something that celebrated sexuality, he penned:

> Take me to church
> I'll worship like a dog at the shrine of your lies
> I'll tell you my sins and you can sharpen your knife
> Offer me that deathless death
> Good God, let me give you my life.

I'm still unsure what this song is about, but I recognize the sentiment, for I have encountered a similar anger. I've come across it in many people. It is folk like this I want my Jesus-faith to connect with. But the chasm is great.

4 8

Language

One day, as I drove out of town, the radio churned out comments and ideas I wasn't interested in. Well, I wasn't interested until I heard one sentence, "All language is symbolic." The radio had my attention now.

I was at pains to know why my atheist, agnostic and sceptical contacts were so confused or dismissive about my faith. I was desperate to know if there was anything I could do about it. I have never been interested in proofs of the existence of God. Even if I could win those arguments (which I doubt), what would that achieve? From what I could see, outsmarting others never resulted in anything of lasting value. Yet there was still a conversation to be had, and I was sure it didn't need to be a religious one. Exploring the idea of language as metaphor might open the door to my enquiry.

However, saying language is a metaphor felt like pulling the rug from under so much of what we think we know when we speak. "Are you saying 'biscuit' doesn't actually mean a biscuit when I say it?" This was stretching my thinking, and I didn't much like it. But I knew I must face up to it.

It is a careful distinction to make, but the actual words are not the thing in and of themselves; they only point to it. So, for instance, we call those furry animals that catch mice and birds and sleep on our sofas "cats". They haven't always been called by this name, and other countries call them something different. My Nigerian friends call them *mage*. To the Spanish, they are *gata* or *gato*.

To take another example, I could say the phrase "peanut butter", but the phrase isn't edible. It is a word, an expression that represents this foodstuff for those like me who speak English.

I know, all this sounds rather bizarre, a discussion just for the sake of it. But bear with me; I don't believe it is pointless. I had a hunch that how we spoke and referred to things was at the heart of the struggle with my embarrassment. You see, if language is symbolic when we talk about the everyday stuff of life, then it must also be true when we talk about God or any religious or metaphysical issue, for that matter. God is not *actually* called God, Lord, Father or any other title. This is symbolic language. Using any of these is always unsatisfactory. The trouble is, words are all we have if we want to talk about these things. To try to be more accurate, we have to use more words.

Geographers know about symbolism. When mapmaking, they say, "Don't confuse the map with the territory." A map is just a representation; it isn't the reality. We could go on. The menu is not the meal; the photograph is not your friend, etc. You get the idea. Well, religious talk is the same.

One twentieth-century theologian, Karl Rahner, proposed that we should stop using the word "God" for 50 years because we didn't know what we meant when we spoke it. Interestingly, many characters in the Old Testament part of the Bible wouldn't use the special name for God (Yahweh) because they knew they didn't know what they were talking about.

I haven't given up completely using the word "God" yet, but I'm tempted.

*

The intrusion of the idea of language being symbolic knocked me sideways. I started to ask myself what I thought I was talking about when I spoke. I asked others what they thought they were on about.

This was another disorientation I had to deal with. I had a sense, though, that I was getting closer to the nub of the matter. But, dear reader, do not lose heart with such talk. Hang in; it is worth the fee!

4 8

Images and ideas

Over eight years in Macclesfield, I visited Beth in a nursing home until she died aged 80. During her forties, she suffered a major stroke that left her incapacitated. I only ever saw her out of bed twice.

Once a month or so, I used to take her communion. We would have a short service, and I'd share something that struck me from one of the Bible readings set for that day. More often than not, she'd asked me the same question, "When we get to heaven, what will we *do*?"

Eventually, I realized why this was uppermost in her mind. For over 30 years, she had lived in the hell of not being able to do much at all. Stuck in her bed, she read a little, wrote the occasional letter, slept, watched telly and enjoyed a rare visit from someone like me. She didn't have enough to keep her occupied. Going to heaven to do nothing all over again was her vision of hell. That would be hell in heaven rather than hell on earth, but hell nonetheless.

Beth never looked satisfied with my answers. There was, though, no easy and quick way to give her an adequate response. You see, it's complicated.

All literature is written at a specific time, in a certain place and within a particular cultural context. That's why I never got on with Shakespeare at school. No one explained why his style, concepts and illustrations sounded so otherworldly. To me, it just seemed like nonsense. I, therefore, dropped English literature.

The Bible seems nonsense for similar reasons. It was written by various men (yes, men) from about 2,000 years before William the Bard. It was written in at least three languages, and we have it translated into another, English. It is no wonder many cannot make sense of it today.

Every age uses imagination in its attempt to describe the world about it. This is necessary when we try to talk about things we do not understand or do not understand well. We have to create an image to help us get our heads around it.

Throughout the hundreds of years during which the Bible was written, everyone assumed that the earth was flat. Why wouldn't they? Look at the evidence they had. It was a fair conclusion to make. If somebody said the world might be spherical, they would have been laughed out of town—and some were.

So, in their imagination, they built a picture of a three-tier universe. As they believed God to be the higher power, they placed him (yes, again, it was all male in those days) high above the sky in the "heavens".

When people died, they buried their bodies in the ground. It therefore made sense to assume the place of the dead was under the earth.

These imaginative descriptions and stories not only helped them to understand how everything held together, but they also carried meaning. They represented bigger, incomprehensible and unknowable ideas.

This is quite a lot for us to get our heads around. Can you see why I couldn't give Beth, who had not been out of her care home for over a decade, a simple one-sentence answer?

An obvious example from the Bible is the well-argued story of God creating the universe in six days. When it was written, most people may have believed it literally; that's fair enough. Some still do today; that's a bit bonkers, but this is not the issue. The creation story tries to make sense of what was around them and express meaning through it.

There was another creation account around at the time. It made the point that the universe was, at its heart, evil and violent. The Jews didn't believe this. So, their alternative creation story stated that everything was fundamentally good. In fact, it went on about this until, in the end, it said, "It is *very* good."

We still use imaginative thinking when we talk about the universe today. For instance, there is something strange about space. It has more mass than seems right. So, scientists created the idea of "dark matter". This is our "fix" for the discrepancy we can't explain.

Also, talk of black holes is quite commonplace nowadays, but we don't know exactly what we are talking about. The Big Bang is our creative way of talking about what happened at the universe's birth. We use these terms and images because there is so much we don't understand. We have so many unanswered questions; we can only speculate. For now, the Big Bang and dark matter fit the bill.

At the end of Jesus' time on earth, the Gospels tell us that Jesus "was carried up into heaven by a cloud". As everyone in those days believed the earth was flat, this made sense. He returned to where everyone believed God lived. However, we've been up in spaceships and know Jesus is not just above the clouds. It doesn't make sense in our scientific age, but it did back then.

These ancient stories do not depend on whether they are historically accurate or not; what matters is what they represent. This one represented the idea that they believed Jesus belonged to something beyond them. This was the only way they could express that belief.

Many who call themselves Christians are unaware of this happening within our texts and within us. Most of my atheist, agnostic and sceptical friends aren't aware of this, and neither was Beth.

So you might see why I have a problem and am embarrassed about what many outsiders think I believe.

4 9

Expressing the inexpressible

Many years earlier back in Birmingham, the churches from across the region organized a big rally in the city centre. A thousand or more folk gathered in Victoria Square by the large sculpture and fountain known by Brummies as the "floozy in the jacuzzi". Speakers spoke, and musicians played. At one point during the proceedings, we were all instructed to turn towards the Council House (called the town hall in any other city) to pray. We were told to lift our hands towards the sky over the Council House and ask God to get the councillors to follow his agenda. Even before we reached this point, that day, my unease had kicked in. But what was going on here?

The gathering was following a directive from the Bible, "Lift up hands toward God in heaven." I guess very few would have recognized we were caught up in the three-decker-universe way of thinking. Here, we were mimicking ancient ritual behaviour. It was what people of the Bible used to do. It wasn't wrong. It just wouldn't make sense to non-church and non-Christian observers who didn't understand imaginative religious thinking. Doubtless, it didn't make much sense to those taking part either, but it felt like a religious thing to do. Which it was.

My prayer was different and desperate. I prayed that none of my atheist, agnostic and sceptical associates would see me there. If they did, I'd have died. Why? Because to them, it would have looked like incredulous religious nonsense.

As a result of this ancient and pre-scientific way of looking at the world, it is not difficult to see how we've arrived at the image of God as "the old man in the sky".

When I stood chatting with Bill in the darkroom of my photography evening class, I could see how he tried to talk about his residual thoughts about faith using some of these commonly accepted ancient Bible ways of speaking. But these ways from yesteryear don't make much sense to many brought up within a post-religious, scientific worldview. These ancient ideas emerged to help people get their heads around stuff they couldn't understand in that era. But they're not always a lot of help today.

*

Even though I'm not a fan of church buildings and despite St Michael's ancient imagery, it was a good venue for the big festivals—Christmas and Easter. The candlelit carol services were always packed. A sense of wonder was present that many non-church people found attractive. It might be the only time they ever turned up in the year, and that was fine by me. The choir would be larger than usual as extra recruits were drawn in. They'd help us sing all the well-known Christmas carols. *Once in royal David's city* was always a favourite. Its words, though, invest in a pre-scientific three-decker universe understanding without any sense of embarrassment or shame, "He came down to earth from heaven." And then a bit later, from *Hark! The herald angels sing* we'd all join in the line, "Join the triumph of the skies!"

At Easter, we'd open our service by blasting out the hymn *Jesus Christ is risen today*, including the primitive line, "Now above the sky he's king, Alleluia!" I knew my non-church and non-Christian friends wouldn't be comfortable singing such a pre-scientific line. But I would sing these with as much enthusiasm as the next passionate believer.

As I boldly turned up at Christmas and Easter to celebrate these two significant events of our tradition, I can almost hear you shout, "How could you be so irrational? How could you express so publicly such a flat-earth mentality? You're bananas!"

I was brought up, though, to live within two worldviews. One is Biblerooted and religious, the other post-religious and scientific. In a sense, I am "bilingual". I can move between these two mindsets with little turbulence or trouble. Once I was through my childhood, I never believed that God lived above the stratosphere. I knew it wasn't true. But it represented a truth, that someone or something was more than I was. I couldn't explain it adequately, but the picture helped me live with what I couldn't fathom. I used the word "God", but that was always inadequate too.

There are many things in life I cannot fathom, yet I believe them to be true. My love within my family is a massive one. I experience this love far more than I can understand it. I rely on various "props" to help me express it and live in it: birthdays, holidays, Christmas parties, Valentine's Day cards, the giving of gifts, photographs of those who live at a distance, our family's WhatsApp group and numerous telephone calls. These are not the love itself, but without these symbols and aids, I'd find it hard to express what I believe to be true and important to me. There's so much in life I cannot fathom yet still need to express. This is why we all need stories to live by. The people of the Bible needed them, and we need them too. Such stories have helped us develop and evolve as a human race. They hold our families and communities together. We cannot live without models and images; they help us make sense of the complex world around us.

So, where do we go from here?

5 0

Creating space

For a long time, I'd been going out of town for most of a day to discover what prayer might be. These escapes hadn't made me any more religious, maybe less so. But I came to depend upon these weekly outings. When I started travelling out from Bordesley Green, I thought I should be back in the parish, keeping on top of my work. But as the years went by, that all changed. I got to the point where I knew I couldn't survive *unless* I left to find a quiet place. Living close to the centre of Birmingham, it wasn't easy to get into the countryside, but, when I moved to Macclesfield, plenty of open space was close at hand in the Derbyshire hills. The paths from Pym's Chair and the circuit around the Goyt Valley were my regular haunts.

When I started in Macclesfield, the demands were many, immediate and often well-voiced. Plenty of people from each of the churches were used to planning, executing and managing initiatives at work. They brought their work brains into the church, which was both good and bad. One of my clergy colleagues said there was an expectation that, by the end of my first six months, I should have made my mark by stating where I thought we should be going as a family of churches.

I worked hard but clung to what I so much needed—my time out each week. From the heights of Pym's Chair, I could see Manchester Airport and, through my binoculars, identify the planes landing and taking off. A few miles east of the runways, I noticed the factory and aerodrome where I'd completed my engineering apprenticeship. The pull of the churches was to get immersed in church-based activities, which meant more religiosity, as I saw it. My old factory, out in the distance, reminded me where my heart lay—with those who couldn't figure out this Christian faith malarkey many of us had given our lives over to.

The Dalai Lama, the spiritual leader of the Tibetans, said that while the West was busy exploring outer space, the East was busy exploring inner space. I was determined not to lose my inner focus, underdeveloped though it was. I had a hunch that prayer was, at its heart, about awareness, but in terms of personal experience, it was still early days.

*

As the rector of Macclesfield, I had to attend some formal events. An official invitation came through the letterbox. R and I were asked if we'd attend the Mayor's Ball. Previous rectors had always been. Even though this was outside our comfort zone, I replied to say we'd be there.

I phoned Sally, the mayor's secretary, to ask what the dress code was, "Would a clean T-shirt and smart jeans be okay?" "No," she laughed, "It's a black tie event."

Formal dress for a clergyman at such a civic occasion would be a cassock and clerical collar. I wasn't going to turn out looking like a monk even if they paid me. As it happened, we had to pay for the privilege of attending the ball.

I went out and bought a black tie.

On the day, R and I dressed up. R never likes being cold, so, on this autumn night, she opted to wear a jumper and a long skirt.

We arrived at the town hall and walked up the majestic central staircase to be greeted by Sally, who said, "Oh my, you do brush up well!" On entering the banqueting hall, I was horrified to see all the men wearing bow ties. Bearing my newly bought black tie, I was dressed as if I were on my way to a funeral. Someone, looking at her pullover, said to R, "What do you wear when it's cold then?"

The evening didn't get much better as it progressed. We were seated on the top table, a round table, along with Sir Nicholas Winterton MP, George Osborne MP (soon to be Chancellor of the Exchequer), the chief executive of the council with her partner, the head of the emergency services and his wife. It felt like we were sitting at a mad hatter's tea party. Everyone was dressed up to the nines; some appeared rather precocious. It all seemed surreal to me; it was hard to take any of it seriously.

Partway through the coffee course, the cream ran out. I blamed Nicholas Winterton for it but said, "Don't worry, I'll go and get more." Leaving the table, I came across a waiter with his back to me. I tapped on his shoulder. As he turned around, I saw that he was wearing a bright blue ribbon around his neck, from which hung a large solid silver star. He didn't have any cream; he was the Lord-Lieutenant of Cheshire. I quickly said, "Oh, sorry, wrong one," and cleared off.

A dozen or so tables were arranged along the hall. In the far corner was a table for the secretarial and caretaking staff. I looked over there rather wistfully; they seemed to be having more fun than me. As soon as I could, I eased myself away from the top table to join them for a few minutes. They were in good spirits for they had had plenty of spirits. They were my sort of people.

R and I endured the over-drawn-out meal and whispered to each other that we'd escape as soon as the ballroom dancing started. As I was not good at dancing, R pointed out there was no need to add further to our shame.

Running down the grand staircase out into the cool night air, we laughed out loud and promised never to attend again. We never did.

5 1

Resisting busyness

Many who lived in and around Macclesfield described themselves as busy—an identity that easily becomes a badge of self-congratulation. While I had a lot to do, I was determined not to describe myself as busy. Though it was tempting, I didn't want to slip into that corrosive mentality. I'd been there before and I hadn't fared well.

After a few years, I joined a woodwork evening class. I love the smell of wood and of working with natural materials. But turning up each week, there was always the anxiety that someone might ask *the* question. "So, what do you do then?" It couldn't be dodged, of course. It is how we make small talk and get to know one another. Sometimes, these conversations opened up the interchanges, but all too often, they closed them down.

One year, a man who was much older than the rest of us joined our class. Because he seemed ancient to the rest of us no one ever asked Richard *the* question. It seems we get to an age when others stop asking us what we do as if we've always been old and retired. Most weeks he was late arriving as he brought his disabled adult son who had severe learning difficulties. His tender devotion to Jeffrey was a delight to observe. Together, they were a wonderful example of flourishing humanity, despite the hard struggle they both endured.

He never advertised it, but Richard was a bishop. At no time did he parade his bishopness. How he handled himself and cared for his son was a better testimonial than all the grandeur he had known during his working life in the church. We didn't need to know his title or see his gold-braided garb. Their strong humility said everything. If there was a witness to Jesus in that workshop each week, it was them. Nothing religious or supernatural was required.

*

Halfway through my ten-year stint in the town, the pressure to work harder intensified. I decided to implement an email policy to help protect my space. Some thought it was draconian. But too much of my time was spent dealing with emails and management matters when my calling was about other things. So, to maintain my priorities, I said I would only deal with emails on Wednesdays and Saturdays. If there was something urgent, I said, please phone me. If a tragedy happens in the town (a jumbo jet crashes on it, for instance), then come and get me.

Much communication in church life had become distant, being transacted, in the main, by texts and emails. My understanding was that a church was a community before anything else. Phone calls would have been far more welcome, but there weren't many. I'd prefer it even more if folk came and spoke to me.

Emboldened by my email policy, I pushed my anti-busyness agenda further the following year. Not only was church life dominated by emails, but also by organizational and business meetings. I proposed to the church council that there should be no business meetings during the season of Lent (the six weeks of preparation leading up to Easter). If there was an emergency, yes, one could be held. But not otherwise. I was astonished that it passed without any opposition. Maybe there were enough people there who wanted similar things to me.

When I suggested the following year that we do the same for the four weeks of the season of Advent, they said that was a bridge too far. Well, I tried.

Why do I tell you all of this? I tell you because I know many non-church and non-Christian people also appreciate quietness, space and reflection in their lives. I never feel the drag of my embarrassment when talking about these things with them. Something awakens in us when we take time out. I know many find a walk in the countryside energizing and life-giving. When we pause, we learn to wake up and become aware. We start to contemplate. Then, we become more human, which I believe is the call of God.

I was soon to learn that children had much to teach us adults about the use of time and the need to play.

5 2

Children in their seriousness

The bishop called a meeting of all the clergy and churchwardens at Nantwich Town Hall. I can't remember what it was all about except for one thing. He asked the gathered assembly of about 300 if anyone had ever been into a bookies to place a bet. No one had. Or no one was prepared to own up they had.

The bishop guessed that someone coming into church for the first time would feel like one of us going into the bookmakers. His point was to encourage us (or coerce us) to make our churches more welcoming to visitors. I thought about this and decided to place a bet the next day to see what it felt like.

When I arrived, the shop was empty except for one man hunched over a newspaper and a woman behind the glazed cashier's screen. I said to her, "I've come to place a bet. I've never done it before; how's it done?" She looked a bit flummoxed. After talking at cross-purposes for a moment or two, she asked if I wanted to place a bet on a horse, a dog or a virtual horse. Now I was the one who was flummoxed. In a slight panic, I plumped for a horse, went to the board where they were listed and chose a name. In my recklessness, I splashed out five pounds and left with a small receipt.

Yes, I could see how the experience of church might be similar in some ways for a newcomer. It was often a similar experience for me when I visited a church I did not know, even though I was part of the firm.

My horse did not win.

*

Being the town centre church, a lot of people visited St Michael's. Among them were parents who came asking for a baptism for their child, which I was always happy to carry out. On the allotted day, they'd arrive all dolled up, looking excited, nervous and embarrassed. The men, in particular, looked uncomfortable; in their shoes, I'd have been the same.

Over time, fewer parents brought their children for these christenings. I thought that those who did come must have some motivation, apart from the strong arm of a mother-in-law.

I wondered what church might look like for these young families if we started from a clean slate. I thought we must do something about this.

Whatever we were to do, it was important that any activity should involve a minimum of religiosity. Also, it must be inclusive, have a gentle integrity about it, and nurture creativity and quietness. It certainly had to avoid what I once heard called the Bastion of Belief: cerebral assent, creedal conformity and compliant behaviour. It should also be centred around children.

On many an occasion, as Jesus wandered around Palestine, he messed with people's heads. His men used to have puerile arguments about which one of them was the best. One day, Jesus must have had enough of this nonsense when one of them came and asked him who was the greatest. Well, they weren't expecting what he did. He called over a small child to stand in the middle of this bunch of grumpy men, and then told them, in no uncertain terms, that they'd never get the hang of what it meant to be great unless they became like this child. They struggled to get their heads around that one, and we still do today.

Christianity, church and religion in all its forms likes to be adult in its seriousness. This seriousness is so dull to many, as it has been to me much of the time. It can also be oppressive and abusive.

When churches try to set up children's activities, they assume kids want to be noisy, busy and running around, as if they need excitement, entertainment and noise. What children seek first, like most of us, is connection.

Children in their seriousness, as opposed to adults in their seriousness, are wonderful. Don't get me wrong, I liked getting my kids wild and excited at home as much as the next dad, while R hid away downstairs. But it is essential that children have times when they inhabit their seriousness. If Jesus was right, then we have something to learn from them.

So, I proposed to the church council that we should start a weekly event centred on children and quietness. Unlike many other things the church often does, no one would be told what to believe. It wouldn't be moralistic. It would be about storytelling, experience and connection; the council agreed.

Because young children tend to get up early, we met every Sunday at 9:30 am for no longer than 45 minutes. We called it the Story-telling Service. Families turned up in all weathers. We greeted them as they came. I used to say hello to the children first; they were always more interesting than their parents.

Once we had all gathered, we sang a simple song and welcomed any who were new. Then, we'd invite everyone to move quietly up to our special place at the top end of the building. It was a large area, often called the chancel by churchy people. A wonderful older lady of the church offered to pay to have it carpeted. She thought the idea of this event was marvellous, so she decided to put her money into it. I could have kissed her. Maybe I should have done.

On the floor in the centre of this special place was a round story mat. As the children entered, they carefully sat around it. Many parents sat with them. Others sat on the few chairs behind.

A Bible story was told using the Montessori method. Sat on the floor, the storyteller would start, having memorized a pre-prepared script from a resource called Godly Play. They spoke slowly and deliberately, and not with any excitement. They didn't look at the children but at the small, plain wooden figures and props on the story mat. As a result, the children didn't look at the storyteller, just at what was unfolding on the mat. The story was everything.

Once told, the impulse of adults is to tell the children what the story means. But this is based on the notion that we know and they don't. The instinct of Jesus was that children had something that we had lost.

Once the short story was over, there'd be a pause. Then, the storyteller would ask some "wondering" questions. "I wonder what you thought of the story." "I wonder which part of the story you thought was most important." "Which part did you like the most?" "Did you feel sad or happy at any point?" The children were free to respond or be silent. Some whispered in their parents' ears. Finally, they were asked where they'd like to be in the story and were invited to add a small wooden figure of a child to the scene to represent this.

All this was followed by a time of silence, an ancient way of praying. Four oak sticks were passed around the children and the adults. When the stick came to each of them, it was suggested they held it mindfully. Guiding them, we said they could be quiet and still, think of someone they care about or were worried about, or say a prayer out loud. It is an amazing thing to see children engaging in contemplation. As adults, we assume they can't do it. The truth is, it is the adults who find being silent and still hard to do.

While still sitting on the carpet, we'd end the session with juice and biscuits, sharing news of the past week and what they were looking forward to during the coming week. To me, this bit always felt a bit like a picnic with friends.

Over the years of running these Story-telling Services, I never once felt embarrassed or awkward about what we were doing. I'd have been happy for any of my atheist, agnostic and sceptical friends to see what I was up to. Even more fascinating, the men who came along never had that embarrassed look on their faces; they never looked ill at ease. This congregation had the highest ratio of men to women I'd seen at any of our services.

As the years progressed, I began to experience how children, in all of their seriousness, had so much to offer. They could see what I had become blind to: wonder, joy and mystery. They were aware in a way that I had forgotten over the years of living an ego-centred life. They had a gift that I wanted more of, and they did it without being religious.

*

It wasn't long before we invited adults to sit in silence for half an hour on a regular basis. Each Friday at 9:10 am, anybody could come and sit quietly in the chapel. Nothing was said or done during this time apart from some words to begin the session and a few at the end. We came together to rediscover and practise this lost art. I needed others to do it with me. Otherwise, I'd find the practice hard to keep.

Back in history, it is reputed that a young monk visited his master, Abba Moses, and asked him for a word. The old man said to him, "Go, sit in your cell, and your cell will teach you everything." It was an odd saying, but I sat with people each Friday who longed to understand the same. Whatever is in front of us, even in a cell, is more than we could ever conceive.

What was even odder, even fortuitous, was that, on leaving Macclesfield, I would spend five years with men who lived in cells. I was off to prison.

5 3

Back to the future

I might not have been well-qualified to become the rector of Macclesfield, but I guessed my story might make me an effective prison chaplain.

Getting out of a job as a parish priest is a complex business. It is best to make sure no one knows. To share such news prematurely allows a sort of rot to set in. Then, it is almost impossible to avoid the lame-duck vicar syndrome as parishioners believe your focus is elsewhere, which it is. This is further compounded if you don't get another position. You are then stuck with the old job, its people and all the attendant issues you never got around to sorting out.

I applied for five posts, travelling out of the parish to York, Salisbury and Bridgend in secret. But nobody offered me a job. One prison didn't even shortlist me.

Despite my eagerness to move on and disappointment with my lack of success, I still had some nervousness about becoming a chaplain as I'd be required to look like a clergyman. I would have to dress the part within a more rigid institution—an institution centred on roles and uniforms. Even at this late stage in my career, that sense of unease about my faith still haunted me. There remained a nagging feeling that I had to be courageous and overcome my shameful inadequacy. Those voices from my past were hard-wired into my psyche. It is hard to get out of your head what others have put into it.

Hoping against hope, I rolled the dice again and applied for another post, this time in Lancashire. I went to have a look around ahead of the interview and I liked what I saw. But I didn't dare to count on it. If this didn't work out, I might be holed up in Macclesfield until my pension fund could supply me with an income. That was not a pleasant prospect, however, as my mojo had run out. I was running on near empty. I needed a change.

Having been unsuccessful in applying for five jobs, I started to wonder if I wasn't very good with application forms and interviews.

I was grateful when an invitation arrived asking me to attend an interview at the Lancashire prison.

Finally, as we drove home from that visit, I told R I thought it had gone well. But what did I know? So, I waited. Weeks later, via the cumbersome Prison Service process, the email came. I'd got the job. I wasn't a hopeless case. Somebody wanted me.

During the ten-week wait for my security clearance, I wondered again what I was getting myself into. Macclesfield had taught me many things, including some big words. I hadn't spoken to anyone about my dis-ease, but I understood it had something to do with cognitive dissonance. Now, there's a mouthful. Cognitive dissonance, I was told, is what your head is in when you hold two ideas or beliefs that don't easily run alongside each other. That was me. I wanted my life's journey to follow the Palestinian Jew Jesus, but I had so much Christian religious baggage that felt toxic to me, even debilitating at times.

*

It was no great surprise to some that I ended up in prison. While never serious, I had committed criminal acts. I knew the smell of it.

Soon after starting this new job, I admitted to the vicar's wife of the church near my old secondary school that I, with a few other lads, had broken into their church hall on several occasions while bunking off lessons. As it happened, she was herself a chaplain at another prison. Break-ins had been an ongoing problem at their church for many years. She and her husband mused whether they should put up a sign that read, "Somebody who broke into this hall is now in jail."

My parents had always had compassion for those who had lived close to the line and those who crossed it. During my childhood, they allowed the "naughty boys" from the local council estate to attend a Bible club they ran in our home for us children. My dad also visited inmates at the nearby jail on his lunch break at the Atomic Energy Authority near Warrington.

When they were older, they took their brand of Bible club into a secure establishment that housed children who had committed serious crimes. Their aim was probably to encourage these children to become

Christians, but even so, they had genuine compassion for these young people and all that had happened to them.

More grimly, my great-grandfather was a prison governor. He supervised executions at HMP Lincoln, no doubt witnessed by the chaplain. It is strange how a family's habits and traditions run down the generations.

Our church in Birmingham found it easy to accommodate those who had fallen foul of the law. Ex-offenders came along and fitted into the rhythm of the church's easy-going and chaotic life. Despite being involved in petty crime, some carried a certain charm, for they too were human.

When Adrian and Becca were of primary school age, we agreed to invite two of these men for Christmas Day. Jeff and Barry were overwhelmed. They hadn't spent Christmas in a home for many years. Their lives were a mixture of make-dos and putting up with what was less than ideal through no obvious fault of their own. Once life starts to fall apart, various human failings feed on each other without great difficulty.

There was a sense that becoming a prison chaplain was, as the old film title goes, a return *Back to the Future*. That is how I judged its rightness. There was no voice from heaven or any miraculous or spiritual sign. There was no religiousness about it. All I had was a strong hunch.

CHAPLAIN

5 4

Chaplaincy

A dark mystique surrounds prison life. The locked gates and high walls not only imprison men and women but also keep hidden the reality of life on the inside. Popular TV programmes about life inside don't do justice to the mind-numbing experience of lives lived in constant fear, in what seems like a parallel universe.

On my first day, I arrived at ten o'clock as directed, dressed in my clerical collar. My new boss, an imam, took me up to the chaplaincy. Staff and prisoners stared at me, not because of how I looked, but because I was new. They were sussing me out, looking to see if I had it in me to do the job. Staff were looking to see if I was just another "do-gooder" who'd be naïve when dealing with serious and dangerous criminals. Or did I have some grit about me? Many prisoners were looking for a friendly face. Some were looking for weakness.

What struck me as I first walked along the corridors was the noise and the smell. There is little in prison to soak up sound or stench.

All the floors were either vinyl or concrete. The sound of men walking, men talking, and men shouting travelled too efficiently along the corridors' gloss-painted brick walls. The doors, made of steel, were impossible to close quietly. Their constant slamming added a brutality that further robbed the place of any chance of homeliness.

The smell was not horrendous. It was institutional, a blend of cleaning products, body odour and paint. I only noticed it for the first few days. Even then, I was starting to become desensitized.

In my head, I always knew I was no better than anyone else. But, now in jail, I had to learn that more intensely. Part of the blight of my disquiet with my faith was the popular notion that religious people think they are better or more holy than others. One of my fellow spiritual directors put it well in her Liverpool/Widnes accent, "We're all in the shit. All that is different is that some are deeper in it than others." There's a lot of talk about shit in prisons.

*

The core team of the chaplaincy comprised Church of England, Roman Catholic and Muslim chaplains representing the largest faith populations in the prison. Other chaplains visited once a week to meet the needs of another dozen or so faith groups.

I don't know of any other place where such a wide range of people who are well-informed about their respective faiths are compelled to work closely together daily. In the other multi-faith situations I had worked in there was often plenty of space for folk to work around each other, even avoid each other. Here, there was no escape because we were locked in together and had duties to fulfil by statute. Such intensive teamwork is not everyone's cup of tea. However, it suited me.

Even though we represented quite different faiths, as chaplains, we were not so different from each other. They had their strange clothing, and mine looked tame by comparison. The Muslim wore his shalwar kameez and prayer hat, the Sikh wore his large turban, the Rastafarian wore his colourful hat and scarf, and the Salvation Army officer had his uniform. We were all bizarre in our own way.

I tried to find out if they suffered from the presence of an embarrassment as I did. They told me that any dis-ease they felt about their faith paled into insignificance compared to the racism they suffered. When they told me something of their stories, I felt chastised about my awkwardness. Alongside their experiences, mine was nothing.

5 5

Relief

Once I had settled into the routines of life on the inside, my greatest feeling was relief. Relief from parish work. Relief from the incessant cycle of demands, responsibilities and challenges. Once, when I mentioned at a party that being a vicar was like living over the shop, one vicar's wife said, "No, it isn't. It is like living *in* the shop." It is true; you feel you never escape it.

As a chaplain, I now worked only 40 hours a week. I basked in the luxury of two rest days well away from work. All my evenings were free. I lived in an ordinary house on a typical street. Nothing marked me out as that public figure, the local vicar in his vicarage (except the vicarage was never mine).

I haven't once regretted my path through life, even though I've had to carry the weight of my disquiet. The benefits were so much more. Living life with purpose and meaning (even if somewhat misguided or distorted at times) is not a benefit most people enjoy. It is a rare and valuable gift.

Having lived in the public's eye for 35 years, I realized I'd lived too long as an introvert in an extroverted world. It hadn't left me unwounded. I coped with the constant gaze of others by closing myself off from them. This is not a rare experience among clergy. It is not rare in other extroverted professions that attract introverts such as teachers, actors and comedians who cannot tolerate too much time in the limelight. So why do we do these jobs? It is as if we need a stage or role to express our withdrawn selves. Without them, we might otherwise never be noticed or appreciated. We cope by retreating into our private worlds to recover and prepare ourselves for the next event, gig, class or public duty.

5 6

Inmates

The jail was a parish of sorts, but different to any I'd worked in before. One half of the "parishioners", the inmates, never went home. Eight hundred and fifty men lived locked behind the 30-foot Ministry of Justice-approved walls. They were guarded, punished, supervised, assessed, educated and cared for by the other half of the "parish", several hundred staff, both male and female. This half went home every night through the extra secure gate in the wall. Every institution, school and company has its own culture. But none is as polarized as a community locked away behind a wall with its haves and have-nots, the free and the incarcerated.

The population ran on a rich mixture of fear, sadness, anger, ingenuity and humour. I sensed this when I first walked onto one of the wings. Every other time I stepped onto a wing or visited men in a workshop, I sensed it once again, as if for the first time.

The relationship between prisoners and the chaplains ran on trust. We were not part of the establishment like the rest of the staff. Our place within the regime was more privileged and nuanced. Not part of the punitive system, we tended to be closer to the men. But trust is a delicate commodity. As that swindler Robert Maxwell said, trust is like virginity; you only lose it once. I had to walk a fine line if I was going to maintain my integrity.

The majority of prisoners were generally well-disposed to us chaplains. We were a source of information, useful items and support they might need. But they could also fear our arrival onto a wing. We were the channel through which they learned news from their families, too often bad news. The shout, "The chaplain wants to see you," made even the toughest inmate blanch.

The jail was home to hundreds of men whose currency was brokenness. They had broken hundreds of other people by what they had done. They had broken themselves, too. And for most, they had been well broken before they embarked on their life of crime. An old saying goes, "Hurt people hurt people." Well, it is also true that broken people break people.

More than a quarter of the men in the jail had been brought up in the care system. When I asked a young man if he had got to know some of the guys during his first week with us, he replied, "Oh Graham, I know loads of blokes here. I grew up with them in care homes."

According to our chief psychologist, more than half of the men had a personality disorder. Even more had suffered from mental health issues while incarcerated with us. Some only started to suffer mental illness once inside, often self-harming.

The men's sadness and despair clung to them like glue, a glue that would not wash off. Rick, a respectable middle-class, middle-aged man, killed his daughter's abusive partner. He came each week to our chaplaincy study group searching for truth. We had many discussions. He helped me as I settled into the jail. In one conversation, he said, "You've no idea what it is like to have killed a man." No, I didn't. He couldn't see how any religionized faith could help him in his despair as he coped with his guilt and missed being with his much-loved daughter. I didn't want him to think the version of the Christian that made me shudder and flinch was the only variant available. I spoke about some aspects of my awkwardness and, for that, I think he respected me.

Others felt no remorse for what they had done. They arrogantly continued their criminal activity inside. In my weakness, I found these harder to listen to and virtually impossible to love.

Most men carried a sorrow. Sometimes, the weight of that sorrow became too much. Many coped the only way they knew, by hardening themselves. David Jarrett reported this way of managing sadness in his book *33 Meditations on Death*, quoting his sister's joke at a family funeral, "Crying is like shitting. It's best done in private."[2]

There is, however, a truth present in her wit. Prisoners told me they only wept once they were locked up for the 12-hour-long night.

I came to understand why men took drugs to dull their pain. I would probably have done the same in their situation. I could also see why they self-harmed. Pain has to go somewhere. I easily scratch my skin when I am tired or stressed. There is a sense of relief and pleasure in doing it until R tells me to stop. Too many told me of their relief when they took a blade and slashed themselves; it made them feel better. I get it. Scratching and picking makes me feel better, but only for a while.

This man I have always sought to follow, Jesus, from a small provincial town, always made a beeline for such damaged and beaten-up people—but not to exploit their vulnerability. Broken people understood more deeply the true fragility of all life. They know this better than us, the more well-heeled people who do not understand so well. It is often only when our lives are turned upside down by loss, illness, betrayal or disenchantment that we might start to grasp it.

Immersed in this atmosphere of pain and sadness, I had some hope. From experience, I knew the line Leonard Cohen penned in his song *Anthem* expressed a truth, "There is a crack in everything; that's how the light gets in." The received wisdom, though, of the dominant Christian culture within which I was nurtured was all about "onwards and upwards". But I knew, from my journey, that the path to wholeness is made up of fateful detours, bad decisions and wrong turnings. In the grimmest of situations, I discovered some hope, not loads, but enough. A different sort of hope can be found in the experience of powerlessness, which, unexpectedly for many, is at the core of the Jesus message. A few prisoners started to realize the power of their powerlessness. It is stupid, but most of us think we are in control. It is, of course, only an illusion.

5 7

Connection

The prison was, of course, a precarious place. Being a high-security jail, it housed seriously dangerous criminals. I worked with many who had short fuses. They had few life skills to help moderate their tempers—it was not hard to consider some of them evil.

Threatening and unacceptable behaviour was handled in several ways. One of them was via a special wing called the "seg". This was not its real name; it was what the staff called it, short for "the segregation unit". The prisoners called it the "block". The press refers to these as isolation wings.

The seg was a high-security unit of 32 cells well away from the rest of the establishment. Most of the men there had become violent, unsafe and difficult to manage. When they'd "kicked off" somewhere else, they were restrained and brought down the long corridors to the unit. One or two were housed there because they were in grave danger of being attacked, even killed, by other prisoners due to the nature of their crime. Cells in the seg were opened with a minimum of two officers. Some men had become so uncontrollable that their doors would only be unlocked with a minimum of four or even five officers. In all the years I worked at the prison, the unit was always full. This was the saddest of all sad places in the prison.

From time to time, a seg prisoner would ask to see me. As I trundled down the corridor, I wondered what he wanted to see me for and if I had the wherewithal to meet his needs. I met with a few men face-to-face, but, for most, I had to sit on the opposite side of a reinforced glass screen. The prisoner may have needed a listening ear. He might have wanted me to find out if his family was all right. It wasn't unusual for the man to be incoherent because of his psychosis or as a result of taking drugs. More often than not, they just wanted to see a friendly face. Sat, glazed off from me, they would talk, rant and make aggressive demands. But most would say they were grateful I had given them my time. Before I left them, I'd always ask if they wanted me to pray with them. They rarely refused. So, I'd ask them to place their hand on the glass screen and place mine on the opposite side to match theirs. I would not say much. I asked them to be still and quiet as best they could among the noises of other men on the wing shouting, swearing and hammering on their metal doors nearby. For maybe two or three minutes, we'd sit in silence. It wasn't uncommon for the man who sat isolated from me to weep. I never asked what was going on. Hardly anything is private in jail. They would tell me in good time if they wished to. Life was too tender and the pain too deep to make such a clumsy enquiry.

There were many special moments in prison, but these were among some of the best. Until then, I never realized how important connection is to us as humans. I had taken for granted the well-connected life I was fortunate, or lucky enough, to enjoy. We all have an intense and desperate need to belong and have union, to gaze into another's eyes. It is foundational to who we are.

R and I are fans of the TV programme *Long Lost Family*. It offers what might be the last chance for people to find a long-lost relative. Each episode highlights the case of parents and their children who became separated shortly after birth, usually due to various social and domestic problems. The baby would then be taken into care or adopted. What always strikes me in these people's stories, and can move me to tears, is when that deep need to belong and find their relative is resolved through a reunion. It moves me because I know this hunger is in me, even though I like to spend a lot of time alone. The drive is intangible. Although many have tried, it cannot be defined or put under a microscope to be examined. To have one's urge for connection frustrated or denied is one of the worst forms of human suffering. This is the greatest punishment of any custodial sentence.

Connections are the place wherein love resides. I once thought that life (and faith) was about beliefs, but now I know it is about connection. My most important human relationships are not based on what I do or think but on what exists between us.

A lot has been said and written about prayer over the centuries. Many words are used in prayers today, too many. The KISS principle should apply, "Keep it simple, stupid."

Today, prayer for me is primarily about connection, not talking. It is about connection with the Ground of all Being, as one theologian described God. It is about connection with Love. We Christians glibly say that God is Love. But what if Love is also God?

Oh, that "God" name is such a problem. It is weighted with so much imagery and baggage that sometimes I have no idea what it means. It is hard to rid myself of that infantile programming fed into my young head many years ago: the idea of a surveillance God, the old man in the sky, even the angry Zeus figure.

As I've told you, I have not called myself a Christian for over 25 years. I also try to use the word God as little as possible. The images attached to this name are commonly a long, long way from street-walker Jesus. If there is some truth that Love is God, then any connection with goodness in it is close to who or what God may be. I prefer to use the name "The Great Love" instead of God.

Of course, prayer can have words. Why shouldn't I express my deepest desires, fears and hopes somewhere? Why can't I be open and honest with somebody? But if prayer is primarily about speaking words, I question the quality of its connection. That'd be a narrow experience of relating.

My relationship with R has plenty of words in it. But again, if it was mostly about talking, there'd not be much depth of connection going on; there'd also not be much love. Rubbing along together silently through life and experiencing ordinary things is the central part of who we are.

As I watched a TV drama a while ago, a man said to his date while sharing a meal in a restaurant, "Look at these old people sitting together saying nothing. Their love must have died long ago." The woman replied, "It may be the case they are so secure together and their love so rich that nothing has to be said."

The prominent doctrine of the Trinity has frightened Christians for centuries. But at its core, it is about relating and connection, so it cannot be defined and pinned down in written words. Even the remarkable, controversial and annoying St Paul echoes this. He used the imagery from a non-Christian poem. It ran, "In him (or her, or them), we live and move and have our being." Whatever we mean by God, the reality is not elsewhere but inescapably present. It cannot be thought, only lived.

So, for me, prayer isn't first about saying words, but being—being with another. Words can be quite unsatisfactory.

Prayer should be much more wonderful and broad because it is about having a sense of being connected to Love, to Life. To connect is to be present.

Looking back, it feels as though I have travelled a million miles since my Sunday School days when we sang, "Oh be careful little hand what you do, there's a Father up above who is looking down in love, Oh be careful little hands what you do."

Today feels like a safer space, even if fraught with unknowns.

5 8

Arrested

A year after I started as a chaplain, I became ill.

I'd had rumbling stomach gripes for years. They could be uncomfortable but never seemed to be serious. Doctors had said there wasn't anything to be worried about. Many a time, they were just an ongoing annoyance. I called them my "tired tummy" syndrome.

One Friday after breakfast, I went back upstairs with my tired tummy to get dressed. As I did, I felt increasingly ill as the ache turned into a stabbing pain. This time, I was sure I was becoming properly unwell. I struggled to get both socks on and thought, "Oh, no, what now?" Unable to move, I phoned downstairs to R and asked her to come up. I guessed it could be my appendix. The tenderness was right where it was positioned.

R finished getting me dressed and woman-handled me down the stairs to drive me to the hospital. I had to wait, of course. Sitting alongside other silent sufferers, my thoughts about whether I was ill or not came and went as my pain came and went. There were moments when I wondered if I was making it all up.

It was midday when the boy-looking doctor pressed his two fingers into my abdomen, making me yelp with pain. The diagnosis was almost complete; a scan confirmed the worst.

It is best to be ill in hospital at the start of the week, not on a Friday afternoon heading into a weekend. Once onto a trolley, I was wheeled up to a ward; the operation would be on the next morning, Saturday.

Everything went as well as I could expect in an underfunded health service. The staff were kind, though stressed.

Recovering the next day, I developed a cough. I could not clear my throat. As staff roamed the ward, they looked concerned and offered me a bucket in case my breakfast reappeared. My coughing became a retching, and the white bucket remained empty. All of a sudden, the retching ceased as my breathing stopped. Gasping and unable to inhale, I fell back onto the bed, desperately pointing to my chest. Staff were called.

The pillows were removed, the bed was lowered, the crash button was pushed, and I thought, "This is it."

The worst of it all was that R saw it all. I couldn't breathe, but I could see. She stood ashen-faced and helpless at the end of the bed as staff muscled their way in.

With a paralysed chest, I readied myself for what might come next. All went quiet. In front of me, I saw a single black rectangle. That sense of reluctant nihilism of my earlier years kicked in. I wasn't scared. I had no options. This was it.

It felt like an eternity, but I wasn't down for long. Soon, my respiratory arrest eased, my breathing returned, and the crash team left as quickly as they arrived.

I didn't interpret anything about what happened as religious. It was an experience of life: being close to death while alive. As many others have commented following similar incidents, it made me think about what is most important to me.

I knew what was important for me. It was connection, connection to those I love. Call that God if you wish. I don't think it much matters. Labels are unimportant, but sensing and experiencing the core of Life and Being itself is.

5 9

Prison staff

If the relationship between prisoners and chaplains ran on trust, the interaction between staff and chaplains started with suspicion and scepticism and only sometimes led to trust. Many officers didn't appreciate why chaplains were in prisons. They didn't understand, in the main, what we were about and had little or no experience of what "faith" might be. They ran on second-hand opinions. We were pigeonholed and stereotyped by popular culture. This was all the stuff that fed my awkwardness and maxed out my embarrassment.

Officers were the sort of folk who would have attended my secondary school. They were the children of the baby-boomer generation, raised to be non-religious. For them, God, the church and Christianity were as incredible as they were irrelevant. They laughed about vicars and tarts parties and shared jokes about bishops and actresses in front of us, in an attempt to offend or belittle us. The more sensitive ones might apologize if they used the F-word while we were in the wing office. Of course, none of this bothered us. But the fact they *thought* it might offend was fuel for my dis-ease.

I worked hard to gain their respect. It took time, almost 18 months, before I started to feel properly accepted. Then, some began to tell me things that surprised even them.

One Sunday afternoon, while quiet, I spent time loitering on the wings. An officer who I'd secretly nicknamed The Fridge, because of his height and stature, asked if I wanted a coffee. He'd hardly ever acknowledged me before, let alone initiated a conversation. I knew he wanted to talk. I knew I had to drink officers' coffee, awful though it was.

Being a big man, his colleagues said he was built like a brick shithouse. He looked invulnerable and behaved as such. As I sat down with my brew, he closed the office door. I knew it was serious. Then, it all came pouring out.

Often in charge of a wing of 130 men, he spent much of his time dealing with men who self-harmed, exhibited complex mental issues and lived unstructured lives. He was at his wits' end. What was worse, however, was his home situation. His daughter and son were teenagers. She suffered from anorexia and bulimia. The boy was depressed and slashed his wrists from time to time. The officer felt he couldn't get away from it. I said nothing. I didn't need to. I heard his whole story; I didn't say anything. I'd learnt that the best way to love is to listen.

Then he told me something else I gathered he'd never told anyone else. His hobby was flower arranging. I was stunned; I hoped it didn't show. As a bit of a side-line, his wife ran a small business making dried-flower displays for weddings and parties, and he helped her out. He told me about some of the jobs they'd done recently. It was like therapy, he said. I had no idea what he thought about God or religion. It didn't matter. There had been a connection, and if God is in the connection, then God will do what God will do—or, to put it in my words, the Great Love will do what the Great Love will do.

There was a different dynamic between the two of us during his remaining months at the prison before he moved on. Something had been said, and something had been shared that could not be unsaid or unshared. There's such a good buzz when you feel so trusted.

In time, a few others felt able to share their pain and struggle. However, I was aware it took great courage to expose the inner workings of their lives while working in such a harsh environment. Some officers never would open up. Instead, they'd say, "Oh, I don't believe in God; I believe in science." Their statement probably didn't sound religious to them, but it did to me. And that is the funny thing about religiosity: people inside and outside of the church have made it into something separate from life, as if it is on a different plane. Church insiders and outsiders talk about "spirituality" as if it is a separate realm. There is only one realm of existence. There is only life. It all belongs together.

Few things help us recognize this. One is Love. The other is death. In prison, death was a close reality.

6 0

Death inside

There are three initials that officers, governors, chaplains and prisoners never want to hear. They are the letters D.I.C. They don't stand for drunk-in-charge, despite that being an offence of many inside. It was far worse. It is the acronym for "Death in Custody".

A few months into my time in Lancashire, I heard those dreaded letters as I entered the security "airlock" of the main gate at the start of another Sunday. The duty governor and a senior officer spoke to me as if to say, "You won't want to hear this, but you have to."

In a panic about all I had to do that morning and unsure what to do about this terrible news, I collected my keys. I was the most senior chaplain present that day.

Everything is grim about a D.I.C. Down on the wing, prisoners were locked behind their doors. They knew what was going on; they'd be aware the paramedics had arrived. The footsteps of unfamiliar staff up and down the landings also gave the game away. They well knew what the hushed tones of officers' conversations with the governor communicated.

Shouting from their cells, some exchanged rumours and suspicions. It was expected because he was old. Or, it wasn't right; the staff hadn't taken his cries for help seriously. Or, he was just a "fish-head"; it would happen sooner or later with the stuff he smoked.

Most of the men were silent, suffering vicarious trauma. The closeness of a death and its often tragic and unnecessary circumstances terrified them. They'd sit staring at their grey-painted walls without any easy answers to comfort them. What most frightened them was that it could easily have been them. To live in jail is to live more exposed to the possibility of your death through poor health, substance abuse, violence or that creeping disease, despair.

Making my way back up to the chapel, I rattled off my Sunday morning services as best I could. But bad news travels fast, and that morning was no different. The mood was bleak and sombre as we sang our hymns and went through the liturgy. There was an undercurrent of menacing anger fuelled by fear and the need to lay blame somewhere, anywhere.

Chaplains spend a significant amount of their time listening to prisoners talk about their concerns and worries. Hearing them express their sadness and anger was always a challenging experience, especially as it was hard to resolve any of these feelings while inside. Grief from the deaths of fellow inmates and family members on the outside built up layer upon layer. Some men were like walking time bombs; it never took much to set a light to their rage.

A few months later, another death occurred, not at night as usual, but during the 90-minute lunchtime lockdown. This disrupted the routine for the wings at that end of the prison.

The depressing and well-oiled processes kicked into action. Paramedics, police and senior staff attended and did what was required: made notes, took photographs and searched for evidence. Then, after the body was removed, the cell was sealed as a possible crime scene, and staff returned the wing to some sort of normality.

That particular day, the staff hadn't bargained for the level of anger on the wing concerning Gordon's death. Prisoners claimed it had been preventable, adding that his pleas for support over weeks had gone unheard and therefore unnoticed. On unlocking the 130 cells of the wing, the rage of a few ignited the anger of the many. In just a few minutes, legs were being broken off tables and equipment wrenched from walls to express their fury and to make weapons to escalate the cause.

Staff quickly hit the green emergency buttons. Officers ran from every corner of the prison, converging on the rioting men. Within ten minutes, all the men had been locked back in their cells. They swore and ranted. Many kicked their doors, and a few trashed their pads. It had been a close call, but everyone was safe. The jail heaved a massive sigh of relief.

After three hours, an action plan was agreed to allow the men back out. Fortunately, the senior officer responsible for the wing that day was Mandy. Well-respected by most, non-confrontational in approach and given to smiling, she was the best chance of a good outcome to the day. Part of her plan was to have a couple of chaplains at the front of the unlocking party as the men were let out of their cells a second time. Annette and I were alone in the chaplaincy, so the job fell to us.

Walking into the wing office, we faced a mass of officers, many of whom seemed to be twice our size. And we were to be their salvation?

It was agreed that only one-third of the wing (one floor) would be unlocked at a time. The prisoners would be allowed out for one hour to socialize, make phone calls or take a shower. They would, however, have to remain on their floor. The delicate situation had to be tightly controlled.

As the mass of us left the office to make our way up the stairs, I felt that mixed sense of fear and excitement. This was serious business. I had to do what I had never done before, something I hadn't been trained for. But also, I was aware of being a valued team member by staff who, in other circumstances, might question the need for us God-botherers.

The two of us stood close to each door as it was unlocked and tried as best we could to smile, listen and understand. The officers took most of the anger, and we stood there in an attempt to defuse this depth of feeling.

There is an unwritten rule in jail that works most of the time: Do not hit women or chaplains. I wasn't sure what this said about us as chaplains, but I didn't care that day. So Mandy and the two of us worked our way around the three branches of that floor. A large group of officers stood on the landing, attempting to appear casual while poised, ready for action.

Some came out of their cells still in a rage. Without opposing their strength of feeling, which would have enraged them further, we carefully and riskily allowed them to vent, blame and curse in the hope that their frightening passion would subside. At times, it looked like the green emergency button might need to be pushed again, but fortune was on our side. The first hour felt like a very long hour. Then we had to do it all again on the next floor.

Heartened by success, we started the second hour with some confidence. It was short-lived, though, when three prisoners on the first spur we unlocked compounded each other's rage beyond what we thought we could handle. This was one of the very few times when I thought I might get a good beating, as a chaplain. From my years at school, I knew what a good beating felt like. But I was young then. Now, I was more vulnerable. I was thankful that brick-shithouse-sized officers were ready to step in if required.

By good fortune, the hour passed without further incident.

As chaplains, we had long passed our going home time. I suggested to Mandy that they wouldn't need us now. But no, it was clear the officers would not let us leave until the end of a third successful hour.

The last floor only housed 60 men. That time everything went smoothly. There was even a light-hearted mood on the landing, where officers looked relaxed.

As clergy, we forget how used we are to dealing with death and its finality. We forget how most people only deal with it as it comes to them via the occasional loss of a family member or friend, or maybe by a rare earth-shattering diagnosis from a medic. It is part of our business to journey alongside those whose lives have been devastated by such bad news. We are midwives of a sort, not helping life come into being but death—death which often arrives as a disturbance and disruption.

I remember the Sunday at the end of August 1997 when I woke up to the news that Princess Diana had died in a car crash in Paris the previous night. I was aware that what I had planned to say to my congregation that morning wouldn't do. I told R to get the churchwardens to start the service; I'd be there by the time I was due to give my talk, a different talk. I knew what my role was. I had to verbalize what I thought would be the thoughts and feelings inside those present. Naming what is unspoken, and even maybe unknown, is crucial for any serious orator. It is often only after the thoughts and feelings have been named that any healing can begin. My task was to offer some hope that was more than empty comfort, that empty comfort which is understandably often labelled as the "opium of the masses". Instead, I drew on stories and experiences we had all known, demonstrating that we have survived the stormy waters of life before—sometimes scarred, sometimes grieving, sometimes wiser for the experience. But surviving, nonetheless.

Deaths in custody plunged inmates and staff into these murky waters. At times, the task of a chaplain, like a vicar, is to help the prison establishment navigate such waters. That is not to say chaplains and vicars know all about this darkness. But hopefully, we have learnt to live a little closer to the unknown and the unsettling, to enable others to do the same.

We also lean into the unknowable aspects of reality during life's "normal" moments, when everything appears trouble-free and joyful.

We have to. But it is while living in these painful gaps of unknowability that our imaginative stories, images, models and ideas become a vehicle to help us make sense of our suffering. It is here that myths (in the traditional and technical sense of this word) come into play to help us find a way through.

Following Diana's death, we went into Birmingham with the children to see the mass of flowers covering the cathedral's grounds. We walked around in silence. In one sense, it was nothing new, just flowers, cards and soft toys. But in another sense, it *was* something new, never seen before in my time. We queued with the crowds to sign the book of condolence and pay our respects. We are far from a nostalgic or emotional family. But her unexpected death touched the deep and unknown in us.

6 1

So long, farewell

My last day in the prison was Christmas Day. It was like any other Christmas for the prisoners, a mixture of delight and utter sadness. Delight because they'd get a proper Christmas dinner with all the trimmings. But utter sadness because they would not see their families and friends. As there were never enough staff on duty, there were never any visits on Christmas Day or Boxing Day.

I led the services in the chapel, trying my best to help them glimpse some light in their darkened existence as I bade them farewell. But I knew some would not fare well. I then toured the wings, saying goodbye, as best I could, to both inmates and outmates.

There were three officers I particularly wanted to say goodbye to. I decided to shock them and make them laugh by giving them a kiss.

There was Will; he was a large man and not particularly good-looking. He gave me short shrift when he first transferred to our prison. He behaved as if I did not exist when I accompanied him and other officers as we carried out our duties in the seg. Being ignored sometimes feels worse than being opposed. But we had to work together. It was only when he started supervising prisoners attending chapel services that he began to acknowledge me. It was then that he started to soften. The day it all changed was the day he said he believed. He never spoke much about what he believed. But, eventually, I knew he was on my side when he defended me from the digs and critical remarks of more hostile staff. It was unspoken, but I knew we had a bond.

When I went to say goodbye to him, he hugged me, and I kissed his flabby cheek. He smiled.

Next, I went to see Jenny, who rarely smiled, a trait I find unnerving in women. Often cold and hard, she mocked me and what I stood for whenever I went onto her wing. I was even a bit scared of her, but I saw a depth in her that intrigued me. Whenever I came across her, I felt it was worth giving her some time. She was a lesbian who'd had a hard life growing up in Liverpool; men had contributed significantly to her struggle. She had good reason to hold me and others at arm's length, especially those she regarded as religious. But a strange thing happened. Her cynicism turned into a sort of friendship, even a respect that transformed what existed between us. We knew something had changed, although, again, it was never specifically expressed.

She was surprised when I gave her a peck on the cheek. Then she gave me a second hug, but she wasn't going to get another kiss!

Then there was Tommy. He was an atheistic Catholic. His philosophy of life was to have the best time you can while you're here and try not to do too much damage before you die. He was the only one who looked quite surprised when I sneaked a sly one. Even though he thought I was nuts following this Jesus from antiquity, he was nonetheless friendly and supportive. He typified for me the many I've come across in life who are decent and good people yet find anything to do with faith, religion or Christianity irrelevant and impossible to believe. It seems they've been forced to throw out the baby with the bath water because of our reluctance to reinterpret and reframe our stories, images, myths and ancient worldviews for our contemporary context.

Tommy would often sit at the back of our Sunday services as one of the supervising officers, frequently rolling his eyeballs as we sang hymns filled with flat-earth images and said our liturgies and prayers shaped by medieval spirituality. I loved people like this and understood why they didn't get it.

Besides the shock value and the humour, why did I kiss these three? I wanted, again, to undercut the typical images and stereotypes that so many ordinary folk have about people like me. I wanted to demonstrate my humanity, not any religious spirituality.

REFLECTION

6 2

A small price to pay

I see my spiritual director every couple of months. Helena is my sounding board, critical friend, listening ear, comforter and disrupter who journeys with me as I pick my way through life.

In a recent session, the topic of this book came up (again). Why, she asked me, is it so important to explain yourself to your non-religious friends? Why the strong passion? Where does it come from? So, I regurgitated my well-rehearsed reasons rooted in my conflicted teenage years, my experience at work and the many times when I've felt prejudged by my atheist, agnostic and sceptical friends.

Then she asked, but hasn't this also got something to do with *your* atheism, *your* agnosticism and *your* scepticism?

The room went quiet for a few moments. Usually, I'm able to give a robust answer when challenged. But not this time. I felt I'd been rumbled. It wasn't that I'd been hiding the possibility; it just had never occurred to me.

I smiled; Helena had spoken a truth.

I recalled the account in the Bible of a father who wanted Jesus to help his son who had been sick all his life. Jesus indicated it was possible, but the man cried out in desperation or anguish (I'm not sure which), "I believe; help my unbelief." That was sufficient for Jesus.

There is a terrible shame among Christians about not believing, as if it's a sin. It wasn't a problem for Jesus. To doubt is to be in two minds, to believe and not believe at the same time. This is me. It is probably you, too.

Living in two minds has brought me to where I am today and it is a more contented place. I travel with less baggage.

*

The German theologian and pastor Dietrich Bonhoeffer lost his life opposing Hitler. He knew about the brutality of life and pleaded for religionless Christianity, one that was honest and straightforward, that avoided clichés, unsuitable metaphors and "in" language. I agree with him, but, of course, I wouldn't call it Christianity. I want to know what a religionless church would look like, along with a religionless Jesus (as originally intended).

Don't label me, though, with the title "spiritual but not religious". That is to be individualistic without any commitment to tradition, history or a community that struggles to make sense of life through dialogue, argument and disagreement.

As well as labelling and stereotyping me, outsiders sometimes also regard me as guilty (by association with a Christian majority) of believing incredible, indefensible and unbelievable things. Making the Christian faith supernatural has robbed it of its humanity, richness and relevance to most people living in a scientific, postmodern and even metamodern age. Jesus invested in the down-to-earth here-and-now reality; any possible future was only conceivable because of life lived in the present.

If faith doesn't make sense here, it doesn't make sense anywhere or at any time in the future.

*

Having read my story, you may wonder what I believe or hold to now.

If you inquire whether I believe in God, you should know I'd immediately respond, "Tell me what you mean by 'God'." Nevertheless, let me stop being so obstinate and give you an answer.

Love holds and bonds everyone and everything together. A French Jesuit, palaeontologist and geologist, Pierre Teilhard de Chardin, said, "Love is the very physical structure of the universe." I call this the Great Love. Again, this is behind St Paul's progressive statement he borrowed from the pagans, "In 'Him' we live and move and have our being."[3] This is the Great Love.

You might ask, is this Love a person? Without a doubt, it is personable and relatable. But to ask if Love/God is a person sounds like an anthropomorphism; it sounds like we're making Love/God in our human image.

When I worked in the prison, many inmates wanted uncomplicated and robust discussions about who or what God is. Elaborating on St

Paul's borrowed statement, I used to explain our close connection with God as follows:

> Living and moving in God is a bit like being a fish.
> I am a fish.
> I am in God, the Great Love (the water).
> This Love is in me, and I am mainly made up of it (water).
> I am not the Great Love (the water), however.
>
> But I am more this Love than anything else.
> This Love (the water) nurtures life while also being the
>   infrastructure in which I exist and operate.[4]

As I hope you are well aware, we must talk about the important things of life in non-religious and non-technical language. All of us (church insiders and church outsiders) need to speak with clarity and honesty. To slip into religious speak only muddies the waters.

*

Do I pray?

I spend time seeking to be present to this Great Love. It is not so different from being present to the love of my family when they descend on us. Their love, after all, is derived from the Great Love.

First and foremost, prayer is an exercise in awareness and connection, more sensed than thought. I gave up the old habit of trying to persuade or coax God to do anything, as if "He" operates from a dimension other than ours and meddles in our affairs. This Love doesn't occasionally break the rules of nature to do something spectacular or unusual, to change or manipulate our reality. Everything is already spectacular; we just don't see it. Love is already here, intricately and necessarily invested in everything. I must, of course, recognize that this God bears some responsibility for the evils and the things that go wrong all about us, together with the many brilliant happenings. I bear this in mind, uncomfortably, as I pray.

If I "pray about" something or someone, I simply express my desires, hopes and dreams in the context of the wonder and confusion I already exist in. There is no one "up there" or "out there" to influence, encourage or coerce. All we desire is here. All I need to connect to is here. All of God, all of Love, is here.

✳

And the Bible?

I grew up with this library of books as my go-to text. It still is; I don't want to change that. It is, however, no longer the "manual for life" I once thought. Instead, it is the record of awful believers and sceptical dreamers struggling with the same questions I grapple with. How can any understanding of God make sense, be taken seriously, or be experienced? The Bible is not full of answers but questions and prompts to encourage us to search. It speaks on many topics with different, sometimes contradictory, voices. But still, there is a wisdom to be mined and a truth to be encountered as long as I read it by putting my prejudices, vested interests and fears to one side and by admitting to my hurts. If we do not take this care, it becomes a weapon for violence or self-aggrandisement.

As this set of conflicted texts with its numerous stories has helped many over the centuries find their way through life, I am hopeful that it will continue to help me navigate my conflicted and compromised life too.

✳

On numerous occasions, the comedian Frank Skinner said it was easier coming out as an alcoholic than as a Catholic. Well, I feel the same. My religion is not Catholic and my addiction is not alcohol, but otherwise I am like Skinner. I live in an unshakeable embarrassment because there is nothing cool or heroic about being a Christian as often portrayed. It's not even attractive to most people.

There is, though, something attractive about the Jesus of the Gospels, unless you're a member of the religious or political elite—to them, he is a threat.

This is why I will remain a follower as best I can; the embarrassment and dis-ease are worth the price for the ride.

And, of course, the ride goes on.

6 3

From surveillance to love

Five months after I left the prison service, I had a great sense that I must go and see my brother. Andrew had been admitted to hospital once again. His long battle with cancer seemed, at times, like his own version of trench warfare. Over the years, he'd received effective treatment and good care and, at times, some ground was gained. This brought him a reprieve to spend more time with Mary and allowed his old cantankerous and witty spirit to return. Then at other times, he felt he was losing the battle. He knew the war couldn't be won, that eventually the fight would be lost.

Just two days after my urge to travel, R and I were on the road to Norfolk, crossing the country at one of its widest points. On our arrival at the hospital that evening, Andrew was vocal, lively and engaging. But by the next day, the illness had got the better of him; he was unable to keep infection and weakness at bay. Sitting with Mary at his bedside, we watched his story come to a close as he slipped from us. His humour, candour and distinctiveness died with him, and we were left behind, watching and grieving. Mary had lost the love of her life and I had lost my partner in crime.

Being close in that chalk-and-cheese sort of way, we had travelled different routes but carried much of the same baggage of disquiet and unease, for we had grown from the same soil. Many a time we had talked about our awkwardness with faith and the church, but I had not been as honest as he had been. Being the more compliant brother, I was inclined to play along with how things were while he was more prepared to kick over the traces.

Love is a strange, intangible phenomenon—but we all know it is real. Without it, life would become meaningless, pointless and ultimately destructive. We do not always find it easy to talk about or admit to except when we fall in love or express it with our children. We feel coy. Andrew and I loved each other but didn't talk enough about this bond that held who we were.

To talk about love in the hustle and bustle of the day can feel weak, just as to talk about God does. Both being intangible, they feel like some of the less concrete things of life, but I know I cannot exist outside of either of them. We are aware of our powerlessness in the face of their strength and all-pervasiveness. I cannot detach God from Love, nor Love from God. In their most untainted form, they are the same thing: inseparable and identical.

As a new friend reminded me, to talk about love in a John and Yoko sort of way is to paddle around in the shallow waters too far removed from deep belonging. This is a utopian form of love, not a love grounded in the gritty and sometimes grim realities of our lives, often polluted by hatred and fear. Like cheap religion, this cheap love doesn't satisfy for very long and soon burns out.

Unfortunately, our lexicon around the word love is very poor. Arctic people have many words for snow and we have plenty of ways to talk about rain. The Greeks had numerous words for love, in all its various forms and expressions. But, in English, we only have one word, and we regularly devalue that.

Recently, after a very difficult day, all the feelings I had experienced when I lost R to the hospital all those years ago suddenly came racing back to me. That night, my sleep was erratic. Feeling unwell and sickly in the early hours, I came downstairs. I thought I was going to vomit. I'd never quite felt this way before and it confused me until I realized what it was: fear. It was visceral in its power. The unresolved experiences of trepidation from long ago broke free from their well-fastened moorings and disorientated me. It had felt like a threat to our love. Both fear and love are not so much thought as experienced and lived. That night I knew both.

God, being Love, is also not primarily thought but experienced and lived. I can think about my love of R, but it can never be a substitute for the real thing. I do think about my life with God (as I continue to develop my theology), but it is not enough. I now know that life is more about what I sense than what I think, although I never want to become irrational or lose my marbles.

Some want to describe this as religiousness or spirituality, but for me, it is merely the fundamental stuff of Life.

My embarrassment has been rooted in the imposition of a religious or spiritual framework onto my engagement with this Life. It has been imposed in such a dominant manner that the framework has all but replaced the original essence that it sought to nurture and support. The New Testament part of the Bible names this essence the "Word" or the "Christ".

I understand why many who have formed the audience of my life (relatives, friends, associates and colleagues) have been incredulous about my so-called faith, for they have not been able to see what is most important due to the obscuring scaffolding. And neither have I for much of my life.

*

Like you, my life started in my mother's womb. She loved me and I lived in that love quite unselfconsciously. I was well-connected. But as the years went by, I had to withdraw from her and she from me. Psychologists call this the process of individuation. I had to learn to live consciously as a person with a separate identity.

Life has taught me that I now have to make the return journey, not to my mother, but to the Great Love, to God, in whom I already live and move and have my being. This, though, is no surveillance God who communicates through haunting propaganda hung on living room walls. No, this is the Life that hangs around in all places, being found in all things and all people.[5]

There is nothing embarrassing about this for it is our wonderful reality.

Notes

1   Author unknown.

2   David Jarrett, *33 Meditations on Death: Notes from the Wrong End of Medicine* (London: Penguin, 2020), p. 124.

3   He also put it another way, saying that everything was in and held together in Christ. But that is to get theologically technical.

4   Graham Turner, *Seeing Luke Differently: Reflections on spirituality and social justice from the third Gospel* (Liverpool: OMG TEXTS, 2021).

5   From the Bible: Colossians 3:11.

www.ingramcontent.com/pod-product-compliance
Ingram Content Group UK Ltd.
Pitfield, Milton Keynes, MK11 3LW, UK
UKHW030210070125
453255UK00009B/160

Deemed 'the father of the scientific detective story', **Richard Austin Freeman** had a long and distinguished career, not least as a writer of detective fiction. He was born in London, the son of a tailor who went on to train as a pharmacist. After graduating as a surgeon at the Middlesex Hospital Medical College, Freeman taught for a while and joined the colonial service, offering his skills as an assistant surgeon along the Gold Coast of Africa. He became embroiled in a diplomatic mission when a British expeditionary party was sent to investigate the activities of the French. Through his tact and formidable intelligence, a massacre was narrowly avoided. His future was assured in the colonial service. However, after becoming ill with blackwater fever, Freeman was sent back to England to recover and, finding his finances precarious, embarked on a career as acting physician in Holloway Prison. In desperation, he turned to writing and went on to dominate the world of British detective fiction, taking pride in testing different criminal techniques. So keen were his powers as a writer that part of one of his best novels was written in a bomb shelter.

BY THE SAME AUTHOR
ALL PUBLISHED BY HOUSE OF STRATUS

A Certain Dr Thorndyke
The D'Arblay Mystery
Dr Thorndyke Intervenes
Dr Thorndyke's Casebook
The Eye of Osiris
Felo De Se
Flighty Phyllis
The Golden Pool: A Story of a Forgotten Mine
The Great Portrait Mystery
Helen Vardon's Confession
John Thorndyke's Cases
Mr Polton Explains
Mr Pottermack's Oversight
The Mystery of 31 New Inn
The Mystery of Angelina Frood
The Penrose Mystery
The Puzzle Lock
The Red Thumb Mark
The Shadow of the Wolf
A Silent Witness
The Singing Bone

The Jacob Street Mystery

R Austin Freeman

HOUSE OF
STRATUS

This edition published in 2001 by House of Stratus, an imprint of
Stratus Books Ltd., 21 Beeching Park, Kelly Bray,
Cornwall, Pl17 8QS, UK.
www.houseofstratus.com

Typeset, printed and bound by House of Stratus.

A catalogue record for this book is available from the British Library
and the Library of Congress.

ISBN 0-7551-0364-5

To P M Stone
Best and Kindest of my Many Kind and Generous American Friends